GLOBETROTTER™

The best of
PARIS

MELISSA SHALES

GW00707837

GLOBETROTTER™

First edition published in 2005
by New Holland Publishers (UK) Ltd
London • Cape Town • Sydney • Auckland
10 9 8 7 6 5 4 3 2 1

website: www.newhollandpublishers.com

Garfield House, 86 Edgware Road
London W2 2EA
United Kingdom

80 McKenzie Street
Cape Town 8001
South Africa

14 Aquatic Drive
Frenchs Forest, NSW 2086
Australia

218 Lake Road
Northcote, Auckland
New Zealand

Distributed in the USA by
The Globe Pequot Press,
Connecticut

Copyright © 2005 in text: Melissa Shales
Copyright © 2005 in maps: Globetrotter
Travel Maps
Copyright © 2005 in photographs:
Individual photographers as credited (right)
Copyright © 2005 New Holland Publishers
(UK) Ltd

All rights reserved. No part of this publication
may be reproduced, stored in a retrieval system
or transmitted, in any form or by any means,
electronic, mechanical, photocopying, recording
or otherwise, without the prior written permission of the publishers and copyright holders.

ISBN 1 84330 836 3

Although every effort has been made to ensure
that this guide is up to date and current at time
of going to print, the Publisher accepts no
responsibility or liability for any loss, injury or
inconvenience incurred by readers or travellers
using this guide.

Publishing Manager (UK): Simon Pooley
Publishing Manager (SA): Thea Grobbelaar
DTP Cartographic Manager: Genené Hart
Cartographer: Genené Hart
Editor: Melany McCallum
Designer: Nicole Engeler
Picture Researcher: Shavonne Johannes
Proofreader: Claudia dos Santos
Reproduction by Fairstep (Pty) Ltd, Cape Town
Printed and bound by Times Offset (M) Sdn. Bhd.,
Malaysia.

Photographic Credits:
jonarnold.com/J. Arnold, page 7;
jonarnold.com/W. Bibikow, page 12;
SC/Gable, page 6;
SC/Chris Parker, page 74;
SC/Monika Smith, page 78;
SC/Geoffrey Taunton, pages 70, 84;
SC/Julian Worker, title page, page 49;
Jaqui Cordingley, pages 14, 16;
Peter Feeny, page 50;
Carlos Freire, page 47;
Roger Howard, pages 21, 42;
Hudson/Shales, pages 27, 33, 53, 75, 76;
Caroline Jones, cover, pages 9, 19, 38, 80;
Gordon Lethbridge, page 28;
Life File/Sally Anne Fison, page 77;
David Lund, page 13;
Norman Rout, page 83;
Neil Setchfield, pages 10, 11, 20, 23, 24, 29,
30, 40, 41, 44, 45, 46, 51, 52, 54, 60, 61, 64,
65, 72, 73, 79, 82;
Melissa Shales, pages 18, 25, 26, 32, 34, 36,
37, 43, 81;
Jeroen Snijders, pages 63, 71;
Stuart Spicer, page 31;
Chris Warren, pages 15, 17, 22, 62.
[SC= Sylvia Cordaiy]

Front Cover: Arc de Triomphe de Carrousel.
Title Page: Notre Dame dominates the Île de la
Cité in the Seine.

CONTENTS

MAKE THE MOST OF YOUR GUIDE

Reading these two pages will help you to get the most out of your guide and save you time when using it. Sites discussed in the text are cross-referenced with the cover maps – for example, the reference 'Map A–C3' refers to the Montmarte map (Map A), column C, row 3. Use the Map Plan below to quickly locate the map you need.

MAP PLAN

Outside Back Cover   Outside Front Cover

Inside Front Cover   Inside Back Cover

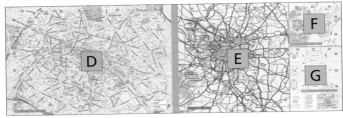

THE BIGGER PICTURE

Key to Map Plan

A – Montmartre
B – Parc de la
      Villette
C – The Louvre
D – Paris City Centre
E – Excursions
F – Disneyland Paris
G – Château de
      Versailles
H – Paris Metro
      Map

USING THIS BOOK

Key to Symbols

⊠ — address   ⊕ — opening times

☎ — telephone   🚌 — tour

📠 — fax   ⏱ — entry fee

🖥 — website   🍴 — restaurants nearby

🖱 — e-mail address   M — nearest metro station

Map Legend

motorway	━━━	main road	**Bd Voltaire**
national road	━━━	other road	Rue du Four
main road	━━━	built-up area	
main road untarred	━━━	post office	⊠
river	Seine	parking area	P
route number	N118	police station	●
city	PARIS	hospital	⊕
major town	⊙ Cergy	metro station	Ⓜ Pigalle
village	◎ Vincennes	RER station	● PTE MAILLOT
airport	✈	bus station	🚍
place of interest	● Parc Astérix	shopping centre	Ⓢ Le Printemps
railway	━━━	library	📖
castle	🏰 Château d'Herivaux	one-way street	→
toll road	Ⓣ	place of worship	△ St-Sulpice
hotel	Ⓗ L'HÔTEL	tourist information	ℹ
building of interest	Archives Nationales	park & garden	Jardin des Plantes

Keep us Current

Travel information is apt to change, which is why we regularly update our guides. We'd be most grateful to receive feedback from you if you've noted something we should include in our updates. If you have any new information, please share it with us by writing to the Publishing Manager, Globetrotter, at the office nearest to you (addresses on the imprint page of this guide). The most significant contribution to each new edition will be rewarded with a free copy of the updated guide.

Above: *The Jardins du Trocadéro and Palais de Chaillot as seen from the Eiffel Tower.*

The Arrondissements
Nineteenth-century Paris was a lawless place and Napoleon III was determined to impose discipline on the unruly mob and the layout of the city. Between 1852 and 1870 his Prefect of the Seine, Baron Georges Haussmann, began to remodel Paris. Among the structures to tumble were the city walls, their space used to create a ring road, the **Boulevard Périphérique**. The area within this circle was incorporated into the **Ville de Paris** and the districts were redivided into 20 arrondissements. The system is still in use today, starting at the heart of Paris, the Louvre, with the first arrondissement, and spiralling out clockwise to the 20th. Anything outside the Périphérique is a suburb. Street signs and maps mark the arrondissement alongside the name.

PARIS

A city of crowned heads and severed heads, with soaring architectural triumphs, from the glorious Cathedral of Notre Dame to the magnificence of Versailles and the avant-garde spectacle of the Georges Pompidou Centre, Paris is superb.

The city has witnessed the fate of kings and empires and has nurtured many of the world's greatest artists, writers, philosophers and musicians. Every age has left a legacy of splendid monuments and gracious churches. Yet the real magic of Paris comes not only from these magnificent creations, but from the shuttered, balconied boulevards, the winding backstreets, the small squares and the avenues of trees.

The Land

It is the works of man, not nature, that have given Paris its unique charm, yet the surrounding landscape, a low-lying plain in northern France, is gentle and fruitful with a light that has inspired generations of artists.

Central Paris, defined by its terrifying ring road, the **Boulevard Périphérique**, covers a comparatively small area of about 105km² (40 sq miles) and has a population of around 2,250,000. It lies at the heart of the **Île de France**, which, in spite of its name, is not an island but defines the tiny area that was the personal domain of the early kings.

The River Seine

Defining the geography, architecture and whole fibre of Paris, the River Seine loops slowly through the city for 12km (7½ miles), languidly accepting all tributes, including its elevation to World Heritage Site status.

History in Brief

The history of Paris is one of death from famine and disease among the poor, of ostentatious consumption among the rich, all stained by the blood of war and siege, riot and revolution. The city has been invaded or besieged by the Romans, Alemanni, Franks, Huns, Vikings, English and, several times, the Germans. The gaps between were filled by home-grown violence, directed usually at an autocratic monarchy with little grasp of the real world. Some important dates include:

c300BC Celtic Gaul Parisii tribe settle.

52BC Julius Caesar's troops defeat the Gauls. Romans build a thriving new city, Lutetia.

AD256–80 First Barbarian invasions.

360 City name changed to Paris.

451 St Geneviève leads triumphant defence of Paris against Attila the Hun; becomes its patron saint after her death in 509.

508 Frankish king, Clovis, defeats Romans. Paris becomes capital of the Christian Merovingian empire.

8th–9th century Charlemagne moves his capital to Aix-la-Chapelle. Empire attacked by Normans (Vikings) in 845, 846 and 861.

885 Count Eudes repulses Norman siege.

987 Hugues Capet declared King of France, founder of Capetian dynasty.

1215 University of Paris recognized.

1253 Sorbonne University founded.

1302 First meeting of the Estates General, France's equivalent of a parliament.

c1310 Establishment of the Parlement de Paris as a judicial court.

1337 The Hundred Years War against England.

Growth of a City
1180–1223 King Philippe-Auguste builds city wall and Louvre
1364 Charles V builds new city wall and the Bastille fortress
1546–59 First quays along the river and first street lights installed
1605 Development of the Marais begins
1627 Île St Louis developed as residential district
1760 Building of Place de la Concorde, the Panthéon and Ecole Militaire
1837 First railway line in France opens between Paris and St-Germain-en-Laye
1852–70 Haussmann redesigns and rebuilds the city.
1900 First metro line
1969 Food market moves to Rungis and Les Halles redeveloped
1974 Boulevard Périphérique and Tour Montparnasse completed

Below: *Not only romantic, but also useful, the Seine is navigable as far as Paris, which has a major port.*

1348 Plague outbreak.

1356 King Jean II is captured by the English, leaving France in anarchy.

1356 Etienne Marcel storms the palace with a mob, forcing the Dauphin, the future King Charles V, to grant parliamentary democracy. Marcel is later killed, and all democratic rights are revoked.

1420 English king, Henry V, occupies Paris and claims the throne of France.

1429 Unsuccessful siege, led by Joan of Arc.

1437 Charles VII recaptures Paris.

1528 François I moves from the Marais into the Louvre, which becomes a royal palace.

1562–98 The Wars of Religion between Catholics and Huguenots split France. Catherine de Medici arranges a truce, gathers Huguenot leaders in Paris and massacres them, together with over 10,000 other Protestants nationwide. War ends when Protestant king Henry IV (of Navarre) besieges Paris, converts to Catholicism to claim the throne, then signs the Edict of Nantes, guaranteeing freedom of worship.

1610–42 Reign of Louis XIII, controlled by Cardinal Richelieu, becomes a golden age of bourgeois prosperity and efficiency.

1643–1715 Reign of Louis XIV, who nearly bankrupts the country with his lavish lifestyle.

1648–60 Several rebellions against the king, including the Fronde.

1682 Court moves to Versailles.

1685 Louis XIV revokes the Edict of Nantes.

1789 French Revolution starts.

1804 Napoleon crowns himself Emperor.

1814 Napoleon is exiled to Elba. Louis XVIII returns to the throne.

1815 Napoleon escapes and marches back to Paris. He is defeated at Waterloo and exiled to St Helena, where he dies in 1821.

1830 A three-day revolution topples Charles X, replacing him with Louis-Philippe.

1832 Cholera epidemic kills 19,000.

1848 Revolution of Contempt leads to the Second Republic with Napoleon's nephew, Louis-Napoleon, elected president.

1851 Louis-Napoleon declares himself Emperor Napoleon III. Start of Second Empire.

1852–70 Haussmann virtually rebuilds Paris.

1870–71 Franco-Prussian War (*see* panel).

1914 Paris escapes invasion during World War I after Battle of the Marne as Paris taxi drivers rally to drive troops to the front.

1919 Treaty of Versailles ends World War I.

June 1940 Government flees, leaving Paris to be occupied by Nazis.

August 1944 Paris liberated. Allies hold back; Free French under Leclerc lead triumphant entry. De Gaulle arrives two days later.

May 1968 Student riots.

1977 Jacques Chirac is elected first mayor of Paris since 1871.

1989 Bicentenary of Revolution celebrations.

Above: *The Eglise du Dôme of Les Invalides, burial place of Napoleon.*

Government and Economy

Paris has been the capital of France for 2000 years and the politics of city and state are inexorably entwined. France is a republic, led by an executive President, who is elected for five years and governs with the aid of a Prime Minister and cabinet. There are two houses of parliament; the law-making *Assemblée Nationale*, elected for five years, and the *Sénat*, elected for nine years, with advisory powers only.

Power in France is largely devolved to the provinces, with the country split into 22 regions, 96 départements and 36,532

The Franco-Prussian War (1870–71)

• Napoleon is captured; radicals take over the Assemblée Nationale, declaring a Third Republic.

• Paris is besieged by Germans; Parisians form a Committee of National Defence. They hold off the siege, but Assemblée Nationale surrenders and Germans march into Paris.

• In the aftermath the committee resists attempts to disarm it and forms the Paris Commune, which is eventually controlled after six weeks of fighting with French government troops, leaving over 20,000 dead, another 25,000 imprisoned and untold damage to the city.

• Paris loses any form of real self-government for the next 106 years.

Above: *A quick coffee and a gossip with the girls – an essential part of 'la vie Parisienne'.*

Parisian Life

Life in Paris is up-beat, fast-moving, exciting, invigorating, and totally exhausting. Parisians pride themselves on being sophisticated, highly educated and well read. They are enthusiastic theatre- and cinema-goers – egged on partly by the lamentable quality of French TV – are willing to discuss new ideas ad nauseam, and keep up a tradition of civil strife, strikes and demonstrations.

Image is all important, whether in clothes, accessories or the quality of the furniture. Fashion swings like a metronome, as people scurry towards the latest trendy district or restaurant. There is a high level of cultural appreciation and Parisians enjoy discussing and philosophizing at length over innovation, especially in art and ideas.

---

communes. Each Paris arrondissement has its own council and administration, and the city as a whole is a département, under the auspices of the *Conseil de Paris*.

Tourism is the city's main money-spinner but visitor numbers are still recovering from the global disasters of the last few years. There are some other money-making industries, most notably **fashion**, with the couturier houses as loss-leaders and spin-offs such as ready-to-wear and perfume making the money, while the surrounding Île de France is heavily industrial.

The People

Everyone knows the clichés – Parisians are haughty and unwelcoming, intellectually pretentious, appalling drivers and terrible snobs. Some are, of course. Certain types do still exist: the well-bred *haute bourgeoisie*, with their drawl and slightly old-fashioned chic; the old-style working class, who survive in small residential pockets in the city and can be seen buying food in the markets every day. However, the city is changing. Many people living in Paris today are immigrants, not only from provincial France, but from all over Europe, Africa and Asia. About the only truism left is that all Parisians know Paris is the centre of the civilized universe and barely recognize the existence of the rest of the world – except as a source of ingredients and for one month a year, during the August holiday, when they spill out of town *en masse* to the countryside and coast.

THE ARTS

Religion

Although the church and state were formally separated in 1905, France is traditionally Catholic and most Parisians pay nominal service to the Church. The influx of North Africans has resulted in a growing Muslim population and there are also representatives of every other faith and cult in the city.

The Arts

Architecture

The 13th-century foundation of **Notre Dame** and **Sainte-Chapelle** heralded in the great era of Gothic architecture that sprung from the narrow, grimy streets of Paris. It was such a success that the city largely ignored Italy's return to classical elegance and only caught up with the Renaissance in the 16th century with the rebuilding of the **Louvre** and **Place des Vosges**. It then swept on to the Baroque, epitomized by the lavish flamboyance of **Versailles**, and an era dominated by architect Le Vau (see side panel), painter Le Brun and landscape gardener Le Nôtre.

The Napoleons added a sombre tone with massive, Imperial neoclassical buildings such as the **Arc de Triomphe**. The Great Exhibitions brought in experimental triumphs in iron and glass, such as the **Eiffel Tower**, **Grand Palais** and **Pont Alexandre III**.

The post-war era has seen an exciting boom in innovative design, with projects such as the Georges Pompidou Centre, Louvre Pyramid, Grande Arche de La Défense, Opéra Bastille and the Bibliothèque Nationale de France.

Louis le Vau (1612–70)
Louis le Vau, the great French architect of the 17th century, was born in Paris. The son of a master mason and trained by his father, his skill first came to the fore in the 1640s when he designed a number of private houses for the wealthy on the Île St Louis. He was then commissioned by Nicholas Fouquet, Louis XIV's finance minister, to design the magnificent château of Vaux-le-Vicomte. His great talents recognized, Le Vau was appointed to work on the Louvre, but it was at Versailles (see page 78) where his abilities ran full rein. There he assembled an unsurpassable team of decorators, painters, sculptors and gardeners to produce the most splendid of palaces for Louis XIV, the megalomaniac 'Sun King'.

Below: *The modern glass pyramid was added in 1991 as the new entrance to the Louvre.*

Sartre and de Beauvoir

Jean-Paul Sartre and Simone de Beauvoir were life-long companions and two of the most influential thinkers of the 20th century. Sartre created the philosophy of Existentialism, which states that existence is basically futile, with no great purpose or meaning. You are totally free to mould and give value to your own life. Simone de Beauvoir's seminal work on the role of women, *The Second Sex* (1949), helped shape the thinking of the early Feminist movement and create a worldwide social revolution. Both were also highly entertaining writers, with a string of successful novels and plays.

Below: *Since students started congregating on the left bank in the 12th century, the booksellers have been ready for them.*

Literature

The intellectuals, and pseudo-intellectuals, of Paris have long regarded ideas as entertainment and words as sexy, lionizing philosophers from Abélard in the 12th century to the 20th-century Existentialists.

In 1634, Cardinal Richelieu founded the *Académie Française*, with its closed membership and closed minds, that has stripped thousands of words from the French language in the name of purity, leaving it much the poorer. The real golden age of French literature began as a frippery, in the resplendent court of Louis XIV, where many bored, wealthy nobles needed constant entertaining to stop them plotting rebellion. The resultant outpouring of fine drama was headed by Molière, Corneille and Racine.

Two authors, Voltaire and Beaumarchais, dominated the 18th century while other philosophical writers included Rousseau and Diderot. The 19th century saw a new flowering of literary genius among the city's novelists and poets, including Balzac, Victor Hugo, George Sand, Gustave Flaubert, Baudelaire, Emile Zola and Marcel Proust.

In the 1920s and 30s numerous British and American authors, including Henry Miller, Ernest Hemingway, Gertrude Stein and George Orwell, headed for the Paris cafés. Depression and war interrupted the flow of ideas and alcohol, but both were revived in the 1950s with the advent of the Existentialists Jean-Paul Sartre, Simone de Beauvoir and Albert Camus. Since then, the banner has been taken up by somewhat esoteric authors such as Alain Robbe-Grillet and Nathalie Sarraute.

THE ARTS

Painting and Sculpture

In the Middle Ages the finest Parisian art was in the stained glass, reliquaries and manuscripts of churches. Secular work was confined largely to furniture and tapestries. However, while in Italy, François I discovered the Renaissance, returning to Paris with Leonardo da Vinci and carts of fine art. His successors grasped the idea but not the quality and Parisian art settled back into fluffy decoration, propagandist statues and second-rate portraits, with exceptions such as works by Boucher, Fragonard and Watteau.

Above: La Siesta *by Van Gogh in the Musée d'Orsay.*

Revolution and the 19th century saw a complete change, as artists such as Corot and Delacroix took to the streets, painting scenes around them with exquisite use of light and colour. They opened a floodgate of new ideas and experimentation. Paris became home to the greatest gathering of artistic talent since Renaissance Florence as artists flocked to the city. The roll-call is stupendous – Cézanne, Degas, Gauguin, Manet, Monet, Pissarro, Renoir, Rodin, Rousseau, Seurat, Toulouse-Lautrec and Van Gogh, to name but a few. New ideas such as Impressionism, Pointillism, Fauvism and Expressionism flourished, but Paris rejected them all and most of these artists lived in abject poverty.

With the 20th century came Cubism and Surrealism and a new crop of artists, including Braques, Chagall, Epstein, Ernst, Léger, Matisse, Miró, Modigliani, Mondrian, Picasso and Utrillo. Until World War II it was crucial for any serious artist to study in Paris. Today the city is still sponsoring new work, but the artistic community is more fragmented.

The Impressionists
The Impressionist painters delighted in conveying light and atmosphere, enjoying colour for its own sake. As a group of artists they are individual in style, but are linked by their interest in painting directly from nature and in developing the theories of harmonious and complementary colour. Inspired by Manet's exhibition of 1863 and disillusioned with the established academic attitude to art, they held their first joint exhibition in 1874. The name came from Monet's painting *Impression: Sunrise* and was used as an umbrella term by a critic to deride the group. There were eight Impressionist exhibitions in all and the painters exhibiting in each varied. Those involved included Cézanne, Degas, Monet, Morisot, Renoir, Pissarro and Sisley.

⊙ *See* Map D–B3   ★★★

THE EIFFEL TOWER

The Eiffel Tower
✉ quai Branly;
Champs-de-Mars
☎ 01 44 11 23 23
🖥 www.tour-eiffel.fr/
teiffel/uk/
✍ relationclient@
toureiffel.fr
🕐 09:30–23:30 (09:00–
00:00 Jul–Aug)
There are usually long
queues; arrive early.
💰 1st stage: 4 euros;
2nd stage: 7.30 euros;
top: 10.40 euros; walk
to level 2: 3.50 euros
🍴 Altitude 95
(☎ 01 45 55 00 21)
Jules Verne
(☎ 01 45 55 61 44)
M Bir Hakeim,
Trocadéro
RER line C, Champ-
de-Mars, Tour Eiffel

Wishing to mark the centenary of the Revolution, the organizers of the 1889 Exhibition looked at thousands of projects
before settling, amidst a hail of protests, on
engineer Gustave Eiffel's iron tower. Work
began in 1887 and was completed in time
for its official opening on 31 March 1889.

The tower is 320.75m (1051ft) high and
sits on four feet, forming a 125m (415ft)
square so perfectly balanced that the pres-
sure never exceeds more than 4kg per cm^2,
the weight of a seated man. It weighs 9550
tonnes, contains 15,000 pieces of metal and
2.5 million rivets. Until 1930 it was the tallest
building in the world. There are 1652 steps
to the third level (or you can ride Eiffel's
original hydraulic lifts), from which you can
see up to 70km (45 miles). Originally it was
painted in graduated colours, from bronze
at the base to a pale yellow at the top.

In 1909, when Gustave Eiffel's 20-year
ticket concession came to an end,
the tower received a last-minute
reprieve from demolition in the
interests of science. In 1914 it was
used as a transmitter, playing a
vital role in the war. In 1916 it
became the beacon for the trans-
atlantic radio-telephone service.
In 1921 it launched French civil
broadcasting and in 1925 Citroën
used it as the frame for the
world's largest illuminated sign.
Today, it is a meteorological and
aircraft navigation station, and
television and radio transmitter.

Below: *The Eiffel
Tower was erected in
the Champ-de-Mars,
originally a military
parade ground.*

THE LOUVRE

The Louvre is not only one of the greatest art galleries, but also the largest royal palace in the world. Allow plenty of time, wear comfortable shoes and don't even try to see everything. It is a sightseeing marathon with 32km (18 miles) of corridors.

Above: *The Louvre is large enough to keep you busy for weeks. Do your homework first and be selective.*

The first fortress was built between 1204 and 1223 by Philippe-Auguste; since then numerous monarchs have extended it. Around the central Cour Napoléon are the northern Richelieu Wing, the southern Denon Wing and the eastern Sully Wing. The most famous exhibit is the *Mona Lisa* (*La Joconde* in French), brought to the city by Leonardo da Vinci, during the reign of François I, who started the collection. By the time the museum opened in 1793 it was one of the richest bodies of art in the world. Almost every great European artist is represented here. Among the paintings, look out for Bosch's *Ship of Fools*; Leonardo's *Virgin with the Infant Jesus and St Anne and Virgin of the Rocks*; Botticelli's *Venus and the Graces*; and Vermeer's *Lacemaker*. Sculptures include Costou's *Marly Horses* and Michelangelo's *Slaves*.

Highlights of the Ancient collection include the *Venus de Milo* (2nd-century BC), the vast granite *Sphinx*, the *Squatting Scribe* (both 4th dynasty, c2500BC), and the Greek *Winged Victory of Samothrace*.

The biggest draw among the *objets d'art* is usually the magnificent 140-carat *Regent Diamond* among the Crown Jewels.

The Louvre
✉ 34, 36 quai du Louvre; pyramid: Cour Napoléon
☎ 01 40 20 53 17
📠 01 40 20 54 42
🖳 www.louvre.fr
🖎 info@louvre.fr
🕑 09:00–18:00 (until 21:45 Mon and Wed); closed Tuesdays and some public holidays.
🚌 audio-guides
♿ Richelieu, Sully and Denon: 8.50 euros (6 euros after 18:00); Hall Napoléon: 8,50 euros; complete package: 13 euros (11 euros after 18:00) Re-entry is allowed on same day.
🍴 contains a variety of cafés and restaurants
M Palais-Royal / Musée du Louvre

Above: *Notre Dame Cathedral is an architectural masterpiece of stonework containing a treasure-trove of carving, statuary and religious artefacts.*

The Cathedral of Notre Dame
✉ 6 place du Parvis Notre-Dame, Île de la Cité
☎ 01 42 34 56 10
📞 01 40 51 70 98
🖥 www. cathedraledeparis.com
📧 info@ cathedraledeparis.com
🕘 07:45–18:45
M Cité

Towers
☎ 01 53 10 07 02
🕘 09:30–18:45 summer, 09:30–17:30 winter

Crypt
☎ 01 43 29 83 51
🕘 10:00–17:30 summer, 10:00–16:30 winter

See Map D–E4   ★★★

CATHEDRAL OF NOTRE DAME

The magnificent Gothic cathedral is the culmination of numerous temples to pagan Cernunnos, guardian of the underworld, Roman Jupiter, and several Christian churches. Built between 1163 and 1330, it is 130m (425ft) long, with 69m (223ft) towers. The spire, added by 19th-century restorer Viollet-le-Duc, along with the gargoyles of the *Galerie des Chimières* and green copper roof statues, is 90m (300ft) high.

The 13th-century west façade has three arches, dedicated to the Virgin (left), St Anne (right), and the Last Judgment (centre). Above is the *Galerie des Rois d'Israel*, ancestors of Christ, Adam and Eve and the Virgin, surrounded by angels. It is possible to climb the 387 steps of the North Tower to see the bells, roofs, gargoyles and views over Paris.

There are three rose windows, each 13m (43ft) in diameter. The oldest and finest, in the north transept, was donated by St Louis in the 13th century and depicts Old Testament figures and the Virgin. The south rose, is dedicated to the New Testament, surrounding Christ. The west window, over the main door, is partially obscured by an organ, one of the largest in the world, with 108 stops and 7800 pipes.

Tiny side chapels surround the towering nave and a magnificent 14th-century carved screen, depicting the Nativity (north) and Resurrection (south), separates the ambulatory from the choir. A door in the southeast wall leads to the Treasury, a collection of reliquaries, statues, books and memorabilia.

⊛ *See* Map D–B2 | ★ ★ ★

ARC DE TRIOMPHE

The top of the Champs-Elysées (*see* page 27) is crowned by one of the city's most familiar icons. In 1806 Napoleon commissioned Chalgrin to design the massive Roman-style Arc de Triomphe (access by subway) as a celebration of his military victories. Fifty metres (165ft) high and 45m (150ft) wide, it was still incomplete when the Emperor was toppled, and was finally finished only in 1836 under his nephew, Louis-Philippe.

At ground level are four high-relief sculptures, the finest of which, from the Champs-Elysées, are Rudes' *Departure of the Volunteers in 1792*, commonly known as the *Marseillaise* (right), and Cortot's *Triumph of 1810*, celebrating the Treaty of Vienna (left). The frieze above also depicts moments of Napoleonic glory, while the arch is inscribed with the names of 660 generals and 128 battles of the Empire. Beneath it lies the tomb of the Unknown Soldier. Stairs and a lift lead up to the roof, from where there are magnificent views. Inside is a small museum.

In 1854, Haussmann surrounded the Arc by a circle of twelve broad avenues, naming it the **Place de l'Etoile**. After de Gaulle's death in 1970 it was officially renamed **Place Charles de Gaulle**, but the name is rarely used.

Arc de Triomphe
✉ Place Charles de Gaulle, Etoile
☎ 01 55 37 73 77
📠 01 44 95 02 13
🕐 09:30–23:00 daily Apr–Sep; 10:00–22:30 daily Oct–Mar
💰 7 euros
M Charles-de-Gaulle-Etoile
RER line A Charles-de-Gaulle-Etoile

Below: *A symbol of France's battles, victories and freedom, the Arc de Triomphe is the starting point for the celebratory annual parade down the Champs-Elysées on 14 July.*

See Map D–D3

★★★

Musée d'Orsay
✉ 1 rue de la Légion d'Honneur for visitors without tickets. Visitors with passes should use the riverside entrance.
☎ 01 45 49 11 11
💻 www.musee-orsay.fr
🕐 10:00–18:00 Tue, Wed, Fri, Sat; 10:00–21:45 Thu; 09:00–18:00 Sun. From 09:00 21 Jun–28 Sep. Closed Mon.
💰 7 euros; 18–25 years: 5 euros; Sun: 5 euros; free for under 18s. First Sun of month is free.
🍴 café and restaurant
M line 12, Solférino
RER Musée d'Orsay

MUSÉE D'ORSAY

The cavernous glass and iron Gare d'Orsay, built by Victor Laloux for the 1900 Exhibition, was once the most central of Paris's ring of railway stations. Saved at the last minute from the crusher's ball, it re-opened in 1986, beautifully converted into a truly spectacular museum of art dating from 1848 to 1914, the period when Paris swept the world.

A sculpture gallery runs through the heart of the museum, flanked by three floors of smaller galleries, showing the development of style from the ground up, with works by Ingres, Delacroix and Corot. The undoubted highlight is the magnificent Impressionist collection, which feels like the best sort of party, filled with old friends – from *Whistler's Mother* to the self-portraits by Cézanne and Van Gogh. Many of the world's most famous paintings are here, including Manet's *Olympia* and *Déjeuner sur l'Herbe*, which heralded the arrival of the Impressionist movement.

Below: *The iron-framed Gare d'Orsay has been converted into a light, spacious art gallery.*

Don't ignore some of the more unusual exhibits, including a room of delightful Toulouse-Lautrec pastels, furniture by Mackintosh and Frank Lloyd Wright, satirical sketches and an architecture gallery. If you only ever visit one museum, this must be the one.

⭐ *See* Map A | ★ ★ ★

MONTMARTRE

A centre of prehistoric sun worship, dedicated to Mercury by the Romans, 129m (423ft) high Montmartre was renamed in the 9th century after St Denis. It is the highest point in Paris, known simply as 'la butte' (the hill).

The huge sugary-white dome of the **Basilique du Sacré Coeur** dominates the skyline of Paris. The architect, Paul Abadie, who delighted in sticking Byzantine domes on everything, let his imagination run riot, creating a magnificent pastiche that has upset most architectural critics, but is adored by those who appreciate late Victorian architecture. There is an excellent view from the steps of the basilica. Inside, Luc Olivier Merson's vast mosaic of Christ swoops over the altar, the heroes of France at his feet.

Montmartre is famous for its years as the focus of the artistic world. Between 1840 and 1920, great artists, attracted by the paintable surroundings, golden light and cheap rents, moved in and created a legend. Many moved on to Montparnasse but their influence can still be seen, such as at **Place du Tertre**, and the **Espace Montmartre Salvador Dali** which has a beautifully displayed collection of art by the master surrealist. The **Musée de Montmartre**, once home to several great artists, including Renoir, Van Gogh and Dufy, now portrays the history and artistic life of the hill.

Rue Lepic is the longest and most gentle route up the hill. At no. 77, the **Moulin de la Galette** (1622), is one of two surviving windmills (out of an original 30).

Above: *The glistening basilica of Sacré Coeur was built by the nation as a mark of repentance and devotion after the Franco-Prussian War.*

Basilique du Sacré Coeur (Sacred Heart)
✉ Parvis du Sacré Coeur, 35 rue du Chevalier-de-la-Barre
☎ 01 53 41 89 00
🖥 www.sacre-coeur-montmartre.com
✆ basilique@sacre-coeur-montmartre.com
🕐 basilica: 06:45–23:00; crypt and dome: 09:00–19:00 (summer); 09:00–18:00 (winter)
💰 basilica: 06:00–23:00; crypt and dome: 09:15–17:30
M Anvers, Abbesses, Lamarck-Caulaincourt

Espace Montmartre Salvador Dali
✉ rue Poulbot

Musée de Montmartre
✉ 12–14 rue Cortot

Au Lapin Agile
✉ 22 rue des Saules

Above: *The monument to the deportees at the eastern tip of the Île de la Cité.*

Conciergerie
✉ 1 quai de l'Horloge,
Boulevard du Palais
☎ 01 53 40 60 97
🕑 09:30–18:30 daily

Sainte-Chapelle
✉ 4 boulevard du Palais
🕑 10:00–18:30 daily
(17:00 in winter)

Crypte Archéologique du Parvis de Notre Dame
✉ 1 place du Parvis de Notre-Dame
☎ 01 55 42 50 10
🕑 10:00–18:00,
closed Mon

Musée de Notre Dame de Paris
✉ 10 rue du Cloître Notre Dame, 4th
☎ 01 43 25 42 92
🕑 14:30–18:00 Wed,
Sat, Sun

M Cité (for all above)

🟊 See Map D–E4 | ★★★

ÎLE DE LA CITÉ

The history of the island dates back to c250BC when the Parisii first settled here.

The **Conciergerie** was once the home of the Roman governor and palace of Merovingian King Clovis. Later, the southern half, the **Palais de Justice**, housed parliament and the Supreme Court while the northern half, the Conciergerie, housed the Concierge and prison. Marie-Antoinette, Madame du Barry and Charlotte Corday were among those imprisoned here. Buildings include the **Sainte-Chapelle** (*see* page 34), the **Tour Bonbec** and the **Tour de l'Horloge**. A tour takes you through medieval halls, kitchens, the executioner's apartments and the cells.

Nearby, **Parvis du Notre Dame** was created by Baron Haussmann. In front of **Notre Dame** (*see* page 16), a brass star in the pavement of this square marks **Point Zéro**, the point from which all distances in France are measured. Below the pavement, the **Crypte Archéologique du Parvis de Notre Dame** offers a fascinating look at the early history of the city, including the remnants of Roman and medieval walls and streets, a Merovingian cathedral and an 18th-century hospital.

Other sights include the **Pont Neuf**, the oldest surviving bridge in Paris (1607), a market in **Place Louis-Lépine** (*see* page 53), the **Musée de Notre Dame de Paris** and the **Square Jean XXIII**, which offers superb views of the cathedral.

On the eastern tip is the **Mémorial des Martyrs et de la Déportation**, dedicated to those who died in Nazi camps.

ÎLE DE LA CITÉ & PARC DE LA VILLETTE

See Map B	★★

PARC DE LA VILLETTE

For over a century this seedy quarter was home to the Paris stockyards, a chaos of live animals, abattoirs and butchers. In the 1960s refrigeration came in and the whole web collapsed, leaving the world's largest slaughterhouse empty. In 1993, a 55ha (136-acre) showcase complex rose like a phoenix, with the aid of architect Adrian Fainsilber. To get there the most enjoyable way, take a boat trip along the **Canal St Martin**, and beyond that, the Canal de l'Ourcq.

The slaughterhouse itself has become the super high-tech **Cité des Sciences et de l'Industrie**, a sparkling interactive hands-on museum designed to keep all ages and people enthralled for hours. The **Explora** (the main body) has two vast floors dedicated to permanent exhibitions on Space, the Earth, the Ocean, Bio-technology, Communication, Mathematics, Sound, Light, Energy, the Human Body and Computer Technology. There is also a **Planetarium** and a special **Cité des Enfants** for 3–12 year olds. The **Zénith**, a huge tent used for concerts, holds 6000 people.

Other attractions include an **aquarium**, the **Géode** (*see* page 73) the **Cinaxe** (*see* pages 73, 74), **Cité de la Musique** (*see* page 72), **Musée de la Musique** (*see* pages 71, 72) and the park itself, which is filled with playgrounds and sculptures.

Parc de la Villette
✉ 30 av. Corentin-Cariou, 19th
☎ 01 40 03 75 75
🖥 www.villette.com
💰 free
Ⓜ Porte de la Villette

Cité des Sciences et de l'Industrie
🖥 www.cite-sciences.fr
🕐 10.00–18.00 Tue–Sat (until 19.00 Sun); closed Mon

Explora
💰 7.50 euros; concessions: 5.50 euros; children under 7: free

Planetarium
🕐 show every hour 11.00–17.00 (except 13.00) Tue–Sun
💰 2.50 euros; children 3–7 years: free

Cité des Enfants
💰 5 euros for 1hr 30 min session (children must be accompanied by an adult).
☎ 08 92 69 70 72

Below: *The gigantic Géode screen.*

Galeries Lafayette
✉ 40 blvd Haussmann
☎ 01 42 82 38 08
🖥 www.
galerieslafayette.fr
🕐 09:30–19:30 Mon–
Sat (until 21:00 Thu)
Ⓜ Havre-Caumartin

Musée Grévin
✉ 10 blvd
Montmartre
☎ 01 47 70 85 05
🖥 www.grevin.com
🕐 10:00–17:30
Mon–Fri; to 18:00
Sat–Sun.
💰 13.80 euros; child-
ren 6–14 years: 9 euros
Ⓜ Montmartre

Opéra Garnier
see page 72

Below: *The central
glass dome of Galeries
Lafayette adds a spe-
cial sense of occasion
to shopping.*

⭐ *See* Map D–D2   ★★

OPÉRA

Between 1660 and 1705 Louis XIV knocked down the city wall and created the Boulevard. From about 1750 the road became a fashionable promenade. In 1860 Haussmann carved out a series of **Grands Boulevards** – Capucines, Italiens, Madeleine, Montmartre, Poissonnière, Bonne Nouvelle, Saint-Denis, Saint-Martin. Together, they now make up a heaving shopping centre, the Parisian equivalent of Oxford Street. Pride of place goes to two department stores, **Galeries Lafayette** and **Le Printemps**. Galeries Lafayette, in particular, has beautiful Art-Nouveau décor. Nearby, is the **Musée Grévin**, a waxworks museum inspired by Madame Tussaud's.

In the Place de l'Opéra sits Napoleon III's magnificently pompous **Opéra Garnier** (designed by architect Charles Garnier), which opened in 1875. The design is a hotchpotch of grandiose styles, covered in relief busts of musicians, classical columns and baroque statuary. Inside, Garnier used multicoloured marble, more statues and lashings of gold leaf. The unexpected highlight, however, is painter Marc Chagall's glorious, swirling ceiling under the dome, painted in 1964. Astonishingly, the largest theatre in the world can only seat 2200 people. The rest is taken up by a vast stage and endless dressing rooms, wardrobes, and workshops which provided the subterranean inspiration for Gaston Leroux's *Fantôme de l' Opéra*. There is a small museum and library here.

See Map D–E5 ★★

THE LATIN QUARTER

On the other side of **Boulevard St Michel**, the area's main shopping street, is a rare surviving fragment of medieval Paris, home to students since the 13th century. Latin was the only language used in the university grounds until the 19th century. Today, its huddle of narrow streets is filled with a multicultural cornucopia of cheap and cheerful cafés, eateries, buskers and boutiques.

Above: *The Latin Quarter's twisting streets and alleys are a multicultural hive of activity and interest.*

The **Eglise de St-Séverin et St-Nicholas** is the official university church. Rebuilt regularly since the 6th century, the existing church is largely 15th-century gothic. The rococo organ was played by Fauré and Saint-Saëns.

The **Eglise de St-Julien-le-Pauvre** was built in the 6th century, but largely rebuilt in the 13th century when it was used as a student hall. It was virtually destroyed during student riots in 1524, and rebuilt in 1651.

Also known as the Musée de Cluny, the **Musée National du Moyen Age** (*see page 39*) is housed in a magnificent mansion built c1500. Beside it are the **Thermes de Cluny**, 2nd-century AD Roman baths.

In c1127 Peter Abélard and his followers gathered to debate in the open air; in 1215 the University of Paris was officially recognized. **La Sorbonne**, founded in 1253, grew into the great university housed today in a sprawl of buildings, which stretch behind the Rue des Ecoles and Boulevard St Michel.

Tucked in among them is the imposing **Panthéon** (*see page 29*), while next door, is the delightful little **Eglise de St-Etienne-du-Mont** (*see page 35*).

The Latin Quarter
M St Michel, Maubert-Mutualité, Cluny-La Sorbonne

Eglise de St-Séverin et St-Nicholas
✉ 3 rue Prêtres-St-Séverin

Eglise de St-Julien-le-Pauvre
✉ 1 rue St-Julien-le-Pauvre

Musée National du Moyen Age
✉ 6 place Painlevé
🖥 www.musee-moyenage.fr
M Cluny-La Sorbonne, St Michel, Odéon

Eglise de St-Etienne-du-Mont
✉ place de l'Abbé Basset
M Luxembourg, Monge

⚙ See Map D–F3   ★★

THE MARAIS

The name 'Marais' means 'marsh' and until the 16th century no scheme to drain and develop the unhealthy swamp really succeeded.

The place only really took off in the 17th century when Henry IV built the **Place des Vosges** (1605). Known originally as the Place Royale, it was renamed by Napoleon in 1800 after the first département in France to pay its taxes. This square is one of the few true Renaissance structures in Paris. Nine identical houses line each side, broken only by the pavilions of the King and Queen. The square was popular for promenading and duels until the garden was created in 1685. Richelieu lived at no. 21; at no. 6 there is a museum dedicated to Victor Hugo, who lived here from 1832–48. A new district for the rich and titled sprang up around the square and the result is a maze of streets and squares, complete with 17th- and 18th-century mansions. There are also several **museums** (*see* side panel), all in palatial houses whose architecture alone is worth a look.

Since the 13th century the Marais has also been home to the Jewish community in Paris, centred on the **Rue des Rosiers**. There are several synagogues and Jewish restaurants in the area. The **Mémorial du Martyr Juif Inconnu** (✉ 37 rue de Turenne, 3rd) has a small Jewish museum.

Rue St Antoine, is an extension of the Rue de Rivoli, based on a Roman road. The **Eglise de St-Louis-St-Paul** and the **Hôtel de Sully** can be found along here.

Musée Carnavalet
Paris in art.
✉ Hôtel Carnavalet, 23 rue de Sévigné, 3rd

Musée Picasso
Superb work by Picasso.
✉ Hôtel Salé, 5 rue de Thorigny, 3rd

Musée Cognacq-Jay
18th-century art.
✉ Hôtel Donon, 8 rue Elzévir, 3rd

Musée d'Art et d'His- toire du Judaïsme
Jewish history.
✉ Hôtel de St Aignan, 71 rue du Temple, 3rd

Musée des Arts et Métiers
Science and technology.
✉ St-Nicholas-des-Champs, 60 rue de Réaumur, 3rd

Musée de l'Histoire de France
National Archives and Hôtel de Soubise.
✉ 60 rue des Francs-Bourgeois, 4th, and Hôtel de Rohan
✉ 87 rue Vieille du Temple, 4th

See Map D–F3 ★★

BEAUBOURG

In the 1960s the poverty-stricken and ironically named Beaubourg (beautiful village) was cleared. In its place, from 1972–7, President Georges Pompidou commissioned two architects, British Richard Rogers and Italian Renzo Piano, to create a globally renowned centre for the arts. The controversial, futuristic, inside-out **Centre Georges Pompidou** fostered a whole new wave of modern design. Take the glassed-in escalator to the 6th floor and work down. As you rise the view expands outwards, while at your feet people swarm around the many buskers in the piazza. The 6th floor is used for major international exhibitions.

The superb permanent collection of the **Musée National d'Art Moderne** covers work from the beginning of the 20th century to the present day on the 4th and 5th floors. The paintings are arranged chronologically but the greatest works, by artists such as Matisse, Picasso, Kandinsky and Léger, are easily accessible in the main gallery. Side galleries are devoted to individual artists or movements. The third, second and part of the first floors are taken up by the Bibliothèque Publique d'Information. There are also performance spaces with lectures, live performances and films.

The south wall abuts **Place Igor Stravinsky**, where Niki de Saint-Phalle's brightly coloured water sculptures, dedicated to works by Stravinsky, create an atmosphere of perpetual carnival.

Centre Georges Pompidou
⊠ Place Georges Pompidou, 19 rue Beaubourg, 4th
☎ 01 44 78 12 33
🖵 www.centrepompidou.fr
🕘 11:00–22:00 Wed–Mon; closed Tue
🎟 15:00 or 16:00 Sat; 4 euros plus museum ticket
💲 1-day pass: 10 euros; museum only 7 euros
🍴 Restaurant Georges; Café Mezzanine
M Hôtel de Ville, Rambuteau
RER Châtelet-Les-Halles

Opposite: *The elegant and architecturally consistent Place des Vosges.*
Below: *The Georges Pompidou Centre contains numerous exhibition areas.*

See Map D–F4   ★★

ÎLE ST LOUIS

Île St Louis was virtually uninhabited until the 17th century. Charles V (1338–80) dug a canal along the line of modern Rue Poulletier, creating two islands, Île Notre Dame and Île aux Vaches. In 1627 rights were obtained to rejoin the two islands and sell land. Streets were laid out and the noble and wealthy were encouraged to buy. Today, the resulting residential area has great elegance and charm.

Amble through the streets and round the quays, breathe in the atmosphere and admire the detail on the fine classical *hôtels particuliers* (private mansions). Many of the houses have plaques that name their illustrious inhabitants. The **Quais de Bourbon** and **d'Anjou**, were originally *the* place to live. A plain façade hides the lusciously decorative interior of the **Hôtel de Lauzun**, 17, quai d'Anjou, 4th (open weekends). Among the artists involved in its decoration were Le Brun, Le Sueur and Bourdon. Gautier, Baudelaire, Rilke, Sickert and Wagner all lived here, while in the 1840s it was home to the *Club des Haschischins* (Hashish Eaters' Club), run by Aglaë-Apollonie Sabatier. The cartoonist Daumier lived at no. 9 on the Quai d'Anjou.

The southern **Quai d'Orléans** and **de Béthune** are now the more fashionable addresses. The Quais d'Orléans offers fine views of Notre Dame. At no. 6 are the Polish Library and the **Musée Adam-Mickiewicz**.

Rue St Louis en l'Île
The following interesting buildings can be found along this main commercial street:
Church of St Louis, designed by Le Vau.
No. 2, Hôtel Lambert, home of Voltaire and Mme du Châtelet; built by Le Vau.
No. 51, the Rococo Hôtel Chenizot, home of Theresia.
No. 31, home of Berthillon, whose marvellous ice cream is a Parisian institution.

Below: *The Quai de Béthune on the Île St Louis offers a relaxed walk by the river.*

Île St Louis & the Champs-Elysées

See Map D–B/C2 ★★

THE CHAMPS-ELYSÉES

In 1667 Louis XIV and André Le Nôtre laid out a promenade, straight on from the Tuileries, through fields of sheep and cows. Extended several times, a drive through these 'Elysian Fields' gradually came to be a popular outing. The real transformation began when Napoleon chose the hilltop for the **Arc de Triomphe** (see page 17).

Above: *No longer a rural promenade, the Champs-Elysées is now a bustling thoroughfare.*

Today the Champs-Elysées is heavily built up with offices and overpriced shops, cinemas, clubs and cafés and few feel inspired to linger. Only the first section, from Concorde to the Rond Point, remains at all Elysian, flanked by trees and parkland.

Nearby, **Palais d'Elysée** is the home of the President of France while the **Grand Palais** and **Petit Palais** caused a sensation with their use of glass and iron during the Universal Exhibition of 1900. Today the Petit Palais houses the **Musée des Beaux-Arts de la Ville de Paris** and the Grand Palais houses the **Galeries Nationales du Grand Palais**, used for major touring exhibitions and the Palais de la Découverte. Until the Cité des Sciences (see page 21) opened, this was the premier science museum in Paris. It now seems a little faded, but is still fascinating.

The **Pont Alexandre III** was also built for the 1900 Exhibition and was dedicated to a new alliance between Russia and France. It is the most beautiful of all the Paris bridges, a joyous affirmation of the Belle Epoque.

Avenue Montaigne is the global heart of *haute couture*, home to many of the world's greatest designers (see page 50).

Palais d'Elysée
✉ av de Marigny

Musée des Beaux-Arts de la Ville de Paris
✉ av Winston Churchill
☎ 01 42 65 12 73
🕐 Closed for restoration until 2005
M Champs-Elysées Clemenceau

Galeries Nationales du Grand Palais
✉ 3 av du Général Eisenhower
☎ 01 44 13 17 17
💻 www.rmn.fr/galeriesnationalesdugrandpalais
🕐 10:00–20:00 (22:00 Wed); closed Mon.

Palais de la Découverte
✉ av Franklin D Roosevelt
☎ 01 56 43 20 20
💻 www.palais-decouverte.fr

Above: *A gilded dome crowns the Eglise du Dôme of Les Invalides.*

 See Map D–C4 ★★

HÔTEL DES INVALIDES

A huge ceremonial esplanade leads from Pont Alexandre III (see page 27) to this massive complex, built as a hospital by Louis XIV between 1670 and 1676.

Designed by Libéral Bruand, it centres on the **Cour d'Honneur**, inspired by the Escorial in Madrid, and housed 6000 men. On 14 July 1789 the mob broke in and stole 28,000 rifles, which they used in the attack on the Bastille.

Behind the court, the **Eglise de St-Louis-des-Invalides** is hung with the flags and standards of France, and those captured from the enemy. The collection is thinner than it might have been; 1417 were incinerated in 1814, to save them from the Allies.

The glittering gold **Eglise du Dôme** (1677–1735) was designed by Hardouin-Mansart as a royal chapel. Several military heroes of France are buried here, but they sink into obscurity beside the splendid **tomb of Napoleon**. He was buried here in 1840, 19 years after his death on St Helena, encased in six coffins, surrounded by the names of his most famous victories. The tomb is viewed from the balcony, to ensure that you bow your head to the Emperor.

The entrance to the **Musée de l'Armée** is marked by an old taxi, homage to the taxi drivers who ferried 7000 troops to the Battle of the Marne in 1914, saving Paris from invasion. This is one of the largest military collections in the world.

The **Musée des Plans-Reliefs** is a collection of beautiful scale models of fortified towns, started by Louis XIV in 1686.

Hôtel des Invalides
✉ 129 rue de Grenelle
☎ 01 44 42 37 72
🖳 www.invalides.org
🕐 10:00–17:00 Oct–Mar; 10:00–18:00 Apr–Sep. Some galleries closed for restoration until 2005.
🚍 offer a variety of tours
👤 adults: 7 euros; concessions 5 euros, under 18 years: free; ticket includes entry to the Musée de l'Armée, Eglise du Dôme, Tomb of Napoleon I and Musée des Plans-Reliefs
🍽 cafeteria
Ⓜ Varenne, Latour-Maubourg, Invalides

⭐ *See* Map D–E5   ★★

THE PANTHÉON

The Panthéon
✉ place du
Panthéon, 5th
☎ 01 44 32 18 00
🕑 10:00–18:30
summer; 10:00–
winter; closed on
public holidays
💰 adults: 7 euros;
concessions 4.5 euros;
under 18 free.
Ⓜ Cardinal Lemoine,
Jussieu

Tucked in among a sprawl of 19th-century buildings in the Latin Quarter (*see* page 23) is the Panthéon.

The first abbey and church here were built in 508 by King Clovis, over St Geneviève's tomb. In 1757 Louis XV began work on a new abbey church for the glory of France, the monarchy and St Geneviève. In the shape of a Greek cross, topped by a huge dome and fronted by a classical peristyle, it was designed by the architect Soufflot and completed in 1789. In 1791 it became a pantheon for the heroes of the Republic. In 1793 Revolutionaries melted down the saint's reliquary, burnt her remains and scattered the ashes on the Seine. Over the next century it became a political football, turning from pantheon to church and back again several times before it finally became a civil building in 1885. Almost every major artist of the establishment of the 19th century had a hand in the frescoes and sculptures depicting the life of St Geneviève, the heroes and saints of France, the civic virtues, and the glorious Revolution.

Heroes of France buried here include Voltaire, Victor Hugo, Jean-Jacques Rousseau, Emile Zola, Soufflot, Louis Braille (inventor of Braille), Jean Moulin (leader of the French Resistance in World War II), René Cassin (author of the United Nations Declaration of Human Rights), and economist Jean Monnet (a founder of the European Community). Marie Curie (1867–1934), the first woman to be interred in the Panthéon, was reburied here in 1995.

Below: *The imposing 18th-century Panthéon is built in the classical style. Built as a church, it is the burial place of many of France's illustrious heroes.*

Opéra Bastille
✉ 120 Place de
la Bastille
☎ Box office:
08 92 89 90 90;
Tours: 01 40 01 19 70
💻 www.
opera-de-paris.fr
🕐 bookings:
11:00–18:00 daily
M Bastille

Viaduc des Arts
✉ 119 avenue
Daumesnil
☎ 01 43 40 75 75
📠 01 43 40 74 74
💻 www.
viaduc-des-arts.com
M Gare de Lyon

**The Cimetière du
Père Lachaise**
✉ 16 rue du Repos
☎ 01 55 25 82 10
💻 www.
pere-lachaise.com
💰 free
M Père-Lachaise,
Philippe Auguste

See Map D–G3 ★★

BASTILLE

Not a trace remains of the Bastille, except an outline in the paving stones of the **Place de la Bastille** and a few foundations, seen from the metro platform (Line 5). Built between 1367 and 1382 to guard the Porte St Antoine, the fortress expanded into a huge castle but was captured six times in seven sieges.

As a prison it mainly locked up those who offended the king, and was nothing like as grim as the Conciergerie. Many of the wealthy inmates had comfortable rooms, good meals and their own servants. The government ordered the demolition of the prison two weeks before the crowd did it on 14 July 1789 (celebrated annually by the French). The **Opéra Bastille** (see page 72) opened in 1989 to celebrate the Bicentennial of the Revolution. Beside it, the **Colonne de Juillet 1830** is a memorial to those who died in the three-day 1830 revolution.

The **Viaduc des Arts** along Avenue Daumesnil has brought a wealth of artisans to the area. Nearby, the **Cimetière du Père Lachaise** is the largest and most interesting of Parisian cemeteries, with a starry list of inhabitants, including artists, musicians and writers, such as Chopin, Oscar Wilde, Jim Morrison (of The Doors) and Marcel Proust. Many of its tombs are impressive monuments and the cemetery is visited as much for its sculptural contents as for its occupants. The Paris Commune made its last stand here on 27 May 1871. There is also a memorial to the French who died in Nazi concentration camps or as a result of their work with the French Resistance during World War II.

| See Map D–D3 | ★ ★ |

PLACE DE LA CONCORDE

This square, laid out between 1755 and 1775 by Jacques-Ange Gabriel for Louis XV, was designed as a promenade – hard to imagine as you dodge the lethal traffic. It is built up only on one side, with two elegant colonnaded buildings; the Hôtel de la Marine (right), and one of Paris' most luxurious hotels, the Hôtel de Crillon (left). To the east are the Tuileries; to the south, the river. To the west, copies of Coustou's superb 18th-century Marly horses mark the entrance to the Champs-Elysées (originals are in the Louvre).

The huge central octagon has a statue at each point representing France's great cities (clockwise from the bridge: Bordeaux, Nantes, Brest, Rouen, Lille, Strasbourg, Lyons, and Marseilles). Within it are two huge, ornate 19th-century bronze fountains, dripping with gods, mermaids and fish, by Jacques Hittorff, and the 75m (250ft) pink granite **obelisk** carved in Luxor c1250BC and given to France by Muhammed Ali, the Ottoman governor of Egypt, in 1831. The **Pont de la Concorde** was completed in 1791 using stones from the newly demolished Bastille (see opposite page).

During much of the Revolution, the Place was home to the guillotine. Both Louis XVI and Marie-Antoinette were beheaded here near the Brest statue. It was given its eventual name of Concorde as a gesture of reconciliation.

Above: *The huge Place de la Concorde has magnificent statuary and fountains.*
Opposite: *The infamous Bastille prison is now only a tracing in the pavement. In its place stand the 1830 July column and the Paris Opera.*

Retail Therapy
Rue Royale, leading north from Place de la Concorde, is one of the richest and most exclusive shopping streets in Paris, a joy for people-watchers and window-shoppers.

| ☺ See Map D–E4 | ★ |

ST-GERMAIN-DES-PRÉS

Since the 7th century, the area around St-Germain-des-Prés was dominated by its powerful Benedictine abbey, cultivating a sophisticated cosmopolitan atmosphere that survives today.

The development of the fashionable Faubourg St Germain assured it a place between old money and radical chic. The Comédie Française flourished on the Rue de l'Ancienne Comédie until forced out by university officials in 1688. In 1857 **Eugène Delacroix** set up his studio at 6 rue de Fürstenburg, now a small museum. Following World War II, the artists' colony, settled into cafés like *Les Deux Magots*, *Café de Flore* and *Le Procope* (which claims to be the world's oldest coffee house, founded in 1686). Customers have included Voltaire, Oscar Wilde, Napoleon, Victor Hugo and Joseph Guillotin.

Today, the area is filled with trendy people and ultra-expensive apartments and shops. Its pavements are tarred because the cobbles were hurled at police during the May 1968 revolt, a fact commemorated in a sculpture on Place St-Germain-des-Prés. Opposite, is the **Eglise St-Germain des Prés** (*see* page 34). The **Musée de la Monnaie**, housed in the old national mint, is dedicated to cash. The **Institut de France** houses five academies of arts and sciences and the **École Nationale des Beaux-Arts**. To the south, is the **Eglise de St-Sulpice** (*see* page 34) and in the square is the 1844 **Fontaine des Quatre Evêques**. On Rue de Sèvres, is the great department store, **Le Bon Marché**.

Musée de la Monnaie
✉ 11 quai de Conti
☎ 01 40 46 56 66
🕐 11:00–17:30 Tue–Fri, 12:00–17:30 Sat, Sun; closed on Mon
💻 www.monnaiedeparis.com
📧 musee@monnaiedeparis.fr
💰 3 euros; free on Sun
Ⓜ St-Michel, Odéon

Institut de France
✉ 23 quai de Conti
☎ 01 44 41 44 41
📠 01 44 41 43 41
💻 www.institut-de-france.fr
🕐 guided tours on Sat, Sun only.
Ⓜ St-Germain-des-Prés

See Map D–E3 ★

LES HALLES

Les Halles opened in about 1110. By 1183 Philippe-Auguste had commissioned the first permanent market hall and was collecting rent and tax from a number of stall holders selling everything from offal to gold lace.

In 1851 Victor Baltard designed a new expandable hall of glass and green iron 'umbrellas'. In 1969 the fruit and vegetable market moved to hygienic, high-tech premises in Rungis. By 1977 only a few street names were left to mark its passing, although the trendy have continued to come here after the clubs close.

By 1979 a modern complex sprouted from the gaping hole. Largely underground, it is mainly a busy, cavernous but uninspiring shopping mall. On the whole, the large park on the roof is the best bit of the new complex. Broken into distinct areas by canopied walkways and pavilions, it has a children's playground and interesting modern sculptures. The western end is marked by the **Bourse du Commerce**, the former granary exchange, beside which is a free-standing column once used by Catherine de Medici and her astrologers (including Nostradamus) for plotting the stars.

The crowning glory, however, is the view of the vast **Eglise de St-Eustache**. The first 13th-century church was built by a merchant. The existing High Gothic church (1532–1640) was modelled on Notre Dame, with an oddly disparate neo-classical façade added in 1754–88.

Les Halles
✉ rue Berger, rue Rambuteau, 1st
Ⓜ Châtelet les Halles

Eglise de St-Eustache
✉ Place du Jour
☎ 01 42 36 31 05
🕘 09:00–19:00 daily (except 08:15–12:30, 15:00–19:00 Sun)
Ⓜ Les Halles
RER Châtelet les Halles

Opposite: *In the square outside the church of St-Sulpice stands a fountain commemorating four French bishops – Bossuet, Fénelon, Massillon and Fléchier.*
Below: *St-Eustache framed by the ironwork of the Jardin des Halles, created when the market moved out of town.*

Above: *The lower chapel of the exquisite Sainte-Chapelle, used by the royal servants, is a masterpiece of vaulting.*

Glorious Glass

The Sainte-Chapelle has nearly 1500m² (16,000 sq ft) of stained glass in 15 massive windows containing 1100 separate scenes. Of these, about 750 are 13th-century originals, the oldest in Paris. The others are superb 19th-century copies. The rose window, telling the story of Revelations, was added by Charles VIII in 1485. Together they make up a pictorial bible. To read them, start in the lower left-hand corner and read left to right, travelling upwards.

Places of Worship
Sainte-Chapelle

The gemlike Sainte-Chapelle was built between 1245 and 1248 by Pierre de Montreuil for King Louis IX (1226–70) to house Christ's crown of thorns and other relics the king had retrieved from Venetian pawn-brokers. The upper chapel, a soaring, triumphant kaleidoscope of stained glass linked by fluted columns, is one of the world's most glorious architectural achievements.

✉ *4 boulevard du Palais,*
☎ *01 43 54 30 09,*
🕐 *09:30–18:30 summer, 10:00–17:00 winter,*
Ⓜ *Cité, line 4.*

Eglise St-Germain des Prés

This church was founded by King Childebert in 542 to house several relics, including a fragment of the True Cross. Sacked four times by Normans in the 9th century, the earliest surviving sections date back to 866, making it the oldest church in Paris, although most was rebuilt in 1193. The abbey remained rich and powerful until the Revolution, when it was virtually destroyed and its library confiscated.

✉ *3 place St-Germain des-Prés, 6th,*
☎ *01 43 25 41 71,*
🕐 *08:00–19:45 (to 20:00 Sun),*
Ⓜ *St-Germain-des-Prés.*

Eglise de St-Sulpice

Work on this huge baroque church began in 1646. Many architects, including Le Vau and Gittard, worked on it but the grandiose façade was added a century later by Florentine architect, Servandoni. The south tower was never finished. Inside are several fine 19th-century frescoes, including works by Delacroix.

✉ *Place St-Sulpice, 6th,*
☎ *01 46 33 21 78,*
🕐 *08:30–17:15,*
Ⓜ *St-Sulpice.*

Eglise de St-Etienne-du-Mont

Founded in 1492, the basic structure is Gothic, but the foundation stone for the portal was laid in 1610, and the façade and much of the interior are pure Renaissance. The few relics of St Geneviève to survive (including her finger) are here as a focus of pilgrimage. Writers Pascal and Racine are buried here, as is the painter Le Sueur.

⊠ place Ste-Genevieve, 5th,
☎ 01 43 54 11 79,
🕐 12:00–18:30 Mon, 08:00–19.30 Tue–Fri, 09:00–12:00, 14:00–18:30 Sat, 09:00–12:00, 14.30–18:30 Sun,
M Cardinal-Lemoine.

Eglise de la Madeleine

Work started on the church in 1764. In 1806, Napoleon commissioned Vignon to build the existing Greek temple as a Temple of Glory. In 1815 the Bourbons turned it back into a church. The classical exterior, surrounded by 52 Corinthian columns and a carved frieze, contrasts sharply with the ornately decorated Baroque interior.

⊠ Place de la Madeleine, 8th,
☎ 01 44 51 69 00,
M Madeleine.

Mosquée de Paris

This 1926 mosque was built as a memorial to the Muslims who died in World War I. Today it is the cultural and religious headquarters of almost 5 million French Muslims. The courtyard is modelled on the Alhambra.

⊠ place du Puits-de-l'Ermite, 5th,
M Monge.

Historical Buildings

Hôtel de Ville

Municipal government in Paris has been centred on the **Place de l'Hôtel de Ville** since 1260. The first Hôtel de Ville proper was designed under François I, but only

The Catacombs

For centuries, Parisian corpses were shoehorned into a tiny corner of Les Halles (see page 33), but the body count rose out of control. In 1780 several people were asphyxiated by the smell. Something had to be done. Work began in 1785. It took 15 months to transfer an estimated two million bodies from the central cemeteries to an ancient quarry, which became known as the Catacombs. Bones were stacked neatly on shelves, and skulls arranged in artistic heaps. The tourists flocked in; the aristocracy held parties and concerts; and the Resistance set up their headquarters in this unlikely place during World War II.

⊠ 1 place Denfert-Rochereau, 14th
☎ 01 43 22 47 63
🕐 10:00–18:00 Tue–Sat; closed Mon.
M Denfert-Rochereau

Hôtel de Cluny

The Hôtel de Cluny, which houses the museum of that name (see page 39), is a fine example of a medieval domestic residence. The heraldic arms of the Amboise family surmount the archway that leads to its attractive courtyard and the house has had many illustrious inhabitants. The young Mary Tudor, sister of Henry VIII of England stayed here after the premature death of her much older husband, Louis XII of France. In the 17th century the mansion was the residence of the papal nuncios, including Mazarin.

Below: *The Palais Royal was rebuilt in the 18th century by Duke Philippe II, but it was his grandson Louis-Philippe who enclosed the gardens on three sides with arcades of shops in order to provide an income.*

completed in the 17th century. It was the headquarters of the Paris Commune during the Revolution and the Third Republic was declared here in 1871. The following year it was torched by communards (see page 8). The current building dates from 1874–82, although the central panel is a copy of the Renaissance Hôtel.

✉ *4 place de l'Hotel de Ville, 4th,*
☎ *01 42 76 43 43,*
M *Hôtel de Ville.*

The Palais Royal

This palace was built in 1624 for Cardinal Richelieu. He left it to Louis XIV, who handed it on to his brother, Philippe d'Orléans. It is closed to the public, but the delightful galleries and gardens are accessible.

✉ *place du Palais Royal, 1st,*
🖥 *www. palais-royal.org*
M *Palais Royal.*

École Militaire

This Classical building was designed by Jacques-Ange Gabriel in 1751, on the instigation of Madame de Pompadour. The military school trained those with no money but good officer potential; its most famous graduate was Napoleon.

✉ *13 place Joffre, 7th,*
M *École Militaire.*

Palais de Chaillot

This vast palace was built for the 1937 Exhibition. The dramatic terraces in front of the building's wings offer the best views of the Eiffel Tower. Inside, the **Musée de la Marine** houses models of French ships, instruments and paintings. The **Musée de l'Homme** is an extraordinary anthropological collection.

✉ *place du*

Trocadéro, 16th,
M *Trocadéro.*

Palais Bourbon

Built between 1722 and 1728 for Louis XIV's daughter, the palace has a classical façade, added by Poyet on Napoleon's orders. Since 1827 it has been home to the French parliament.
✉ *33 quai d'Orsay, 7th,*
M *Assemblée-Nationale.*

Museums & Galleries
Musée Carnavalet

Housed in the Hôtel Carnavalet (1548) which was altered by Mansart between 1655 and 1660, this museum is dedicated to the history of Paris as told through art. Exhibits include several complete rooms, including the suite of Madame de Sévigné; Marcel Proust's bedroom; the Art Nouveau Fouquet jewellery boutique; and the 1924 ballroom of the Hôtel Wendel, painted by José-María Sert. There is also a

model of Paris in 1527, a model of the Bastille carved from one of its stones, a toy guillotine, and a room of shop signs. The paintings document almost every important person and event in the history of the city.
✉ *23 rue de Sévigné, 3rd,*
☎ *01 44 59 58 58,*
🕐 *10:00–18:00, closed Mon and public holidays.*

Musée Picasso

Housed in the Hôtel Salé, built in 1656 by Jean Boullier, is a superb collection of work by Pablo (1881–1973), donated to the state in lieu of inheritance tax. There are few major works, and every period is represented in 200 paintings, 3000 drawings

Above: *The Palais de Chaillot is built as two curved wings either side of a terrace and adorned with the work of many sculptors.*

Sightseeing
Few sights are free, and tickets can be expensive. Buy a ticket for one leg, or whole circuit. Occasional discounts of up to 50 per cent are available for visitors with ISIC (international student) cards or Paris Visite tickets (which also cover transport). The best option is to buy a **Carte Musées-Monuments**. This 1, 3 or 5-day pass gives entry to over 60 different monuments and museums, including all the most famous. Recoup the cost in 3–4 visits and avoid horrendous queues at major sights. On sale at all participating museums and monuments, tourist offices and main metro stations.

Minor Art Museums

Musée National Delacroix
Studio museum of the romantic painter.
✉ 6 pl Fürstenberg, 6th
M St-Germain-des-Prés

Musée Bourdelle
House and workshop of Antoine Bourdelle.
✉ 18 rue Antoine Bourdelle, 15th
M Falguière

Musée Dapper
Fine African art.
✉ 35bis rue Paul Valéry, 16th
M Etoile

Musée National Jean-Jaques Henner
Over 700 paintings and drawings by Henner.
✉ 43 av de Villers, 17th
M Monceau

Musée Gustave Moreau
Moreau's studio, filled with his works.
✉ 14 rue de la Rochefoucauld, 9th
M Trinité

and engravings, and every medium from ceramics to illustrated manuscripts. There is also a sculpture garden, an audiovisual room and a gallery dedicated to Picasso's own collection, with works by Braque, Cézanne, Matisse and Rousseau.
✉ Hôtel Salé, 5 rue de Thorigny, 3rd,
☎ 01 42 71 25 21,
🕑 09:30–18:00 Apr–Sep; to 17:30 Oct–Mar; closed Sun–Tue,
M St-Paul.

Musée d'Art Moderne de la Ville de Paris

This museum kicks off triumphantly with Raoul Dufy's La Fée Electricité, the largest picture in the world, created, like the building itself, for the 1937 World Exhibition. Numerous other modern masters make this a fitting companion to the Pompidou Centre.
✉ 16th Palais de Tokyo, 11 av du Président Wilson,
☎ 01 53 67 40 00,
🕑 10:00–17:30 Tue–Fri, 10:00–18:45 Sat–Sun, closed Mon,
M Alma-Marceau.

Musée Marmottan – Claude Monet

This family collection includes many superb Monets and other Impressionists as well as medieval and Napoleonic furniture and art, and a magnificent collection of illuminated manuscripts.
✉ 2 rue Louis-Boilly, 16th,
☎ 01 44 96 50 33,
🖳 www.marmottan.com
🕑 10:00–18:00 (closed Mon), last entry 17:30,
M La Muette.

Musée Rodin

Auguste Rodin was so successful that he was offered the beautiful Hôtel Biron on condi-

MUSEUMS & GALLERIES

tion that he left his work to the state. The resulting museum is small and immensely satisfying. The salons and gardens are filled with works by the sculptor, including such famous pieces as *The Kiss*, *The Thinker*, *The Burghers of Calais* and the *Gates of Hell*.

⊠ *77 rue de Varenne, 7th,*

☎ *01 44 18 61 10,*

🖳 *www. musee-rodin.fr*

🕓 *09:30–17:45 (last entry 17:15) Apr–Sep, 09:30–16:45 (last entry 16:15) Oct–Mar; closed Mon,*

M *Varenne.*

Musée de Cluny

Also called the **Musée National du Moyen Age**, this museum is housed in a magnificent mansion built c.1500 by Jacques d'Amboise. Inside is the superb national collection of medieval art and artefacts, founded by Alexandre de Sommerard in 1832. It is a treasure-trove of crowns and

reliquaries, carvings, paintings, tapestries, stained glass, illuminated manuscripts, stone capitals and heavy blackened furniture. In Salle VIII on the ground floor are the 28 heads of the Kings of Judea from Notre Dame, beheaded in 1793 by Revolutionaries who believed them to be the kings of France. Salle XII, the frigidarium of the Roman baths, contains the 16th-century Grape Harvest Tapestry. In Salle XIII, the six sublime *millefleurs* tapestries depicting *La Dame à la Licorne* (The Lady and the Unicorn), woven near Aubusson in the 15th century and rescued from a dusty attic 400 years later.

⊠ *6 place Paul Painlevé, 5th,*

☎ *01 53 73 78 00,*

🖳 *www. musee-moyenage.fr*

🕓 *09:30–17:45, closed Tue,*

M *Cluny-La Sorbonne, St Michel, Odéon.*

North of the Champs-Elysees
A cluster of museums is on Place St-Augustin:

Musée Jacquemart-André
Italian Renaissance and 17th–18th century Flemish and French art.
⊠ 158 boulevard Haussmann, 8th
M St-Philippe-du-Roule, Miromesnil

Musée Cernuschi
Chinese and Japanese art through the ages.
⊠ 7 av Vélasquez, 8th
M Monceau, Villiers

Musée de Nissim de Camondo
Superb carpets, 18th-century furniture and *objets d'art*.
⊠ 63 rue Monceau, 8th
M Villiers, Monceau

Musée de la Contrefaçon
Fakes and forgeries, from 200BC to present.
⊠ 16 rue de la Faisanderie, 16th
M Porte Dauphine

Opposite: *Rodin chose a wonderfully romantic house and garden for his studio, now greatly improved by his fine sculptures.*

Jardin des Plantes

This garden was originally laid out as a medicinal herb garden in 1626 by Jean Hérouard and Guy de la Brosse, court physicians to Louis XIII. They also founded schools of botany, natural history and pharmacy which have mutated into a magnificent botanical garden. Buffon, the naturalist, was superintendent here between 1739 and 1788.
✉ pl Valhubert, 57 rue Buffon 5th
☎ 01 40 79 30 00
🕓 daily, 07:15–sunset. Various greenhouses and galleries have shorter opening hours.
🛇 free
Ⓜ Jussieu, Gare d'Austerlitz

Below: *The Jardin du Luxembourg is a popular recreation ground.*

Parks & Gardens
Jardin du Luxembourg

Originally created for Marie de Medici in 1613, these formal gardens were re-landscaped by Chalgrin in the 19th century. Today lined with benches and fine sculptures, they are a regular student hang-out. At the north end is the **Palais du Luxembourg**, again built for Marie and altered by Chalgrin. It is now home to the Senate and is only open for visits to the gallery when the house is sitting.
✉ *boulevard St Michel, 6th,*
RER *Luxembourg.*

Jardin des Tuileries

In 1560 Cathérine de Medici bought a derelict tile works (*tuileries*) and laid out the first gardens. They were redesigned by Le Nôtre in 1664 and still follow his formal plan. The real point of gaiety is the Octagonal Basin, a large pond surrounded by a phalanx of ice-cream sellers, where generations of children have sailed their toy boats.
✉ *between the Louvre and Place de la Concorde,*
Ⓜ *Concorde, Tuileries, Palais-Royal.*

Parc des Buttes Chaumont

In 1860 Haussmann turned a deserted quarry and rubbish dump into this delightful park with tumbling water, cliffs and lavish greenery.
✉ *rue Manin, 19th,*
🕓 *07:00–21:00 daily (to 22:00 or 23:00 in high summer),*
Ⓜ *Botzaris, Buttes Chaumont.*

ACTIVITIES
Sport and Recreation

Parisians are starting to take a greater interest in sport than ever before – perhaps due to their winning the soccer World Cup in 1998, the World Handball Championships in 2001, or the increasingly strong possibility of hosting the 2012 Olympics. During the 2008 bidding process, the Parisian authorities invested in a number of sporting facilities and, as a result, a variety of activities, from canoeing to swimming, jogging, tennis and squash, are possible within the city.

Above: *Boules is more a national passion than a pastime.*

A free book, *Le Guide du Sport à Paris*, available from most tourist offices and town halls, provides a list of sporting facilities, cycling routes and sporting events. Information is also available from **Allô-Sports Services**.

Boules is a classic French game, similar to bowls but played in a smaller area, on rougher terrain and with a metal ball. Popular locations include the Bois de Vincennes, Arènes de Lutèce and Champs de Mars.

Cycling has become popular, mainly due to the new network of cycling lanes that has been implemented (*see Le Guide du Sport a Paris* for routes). The best places for cycling in Paris are the two main parks – **Bois de Boulogne** (*see page 80*) and **Bois de Vincennes**. For rentals *see* page 49; for clubs contact the **Fédération Française de Cyclotourisme**.

In-line skating is also popular. On Friday nights a large number of experienced skaters gather at place de L'Italie to participate in a 40km (25-mile) circuit of the city.

Allô-Sports Services
☎ 08 20 00 75 75
🕐 10:30–17:00, Mon–Fri

Fédération Française de Cyclisme
☎ 01 44 16 88 88
🖥 www.ffc.fr

In-line Skating
Bike 'n Roller
✉ Invalides Esplanade, 38 rue Fabert
☎ 01 45 50 38 27
🖥 www.bikenroller.fr
🕐 10:00–19:30 Mon–Sat, 10:00–19:00 Sun

Rollerparc Avenue
Europe's largest indoor rollerskating centre.
✉ 100 rue Léon-Geoffroy, Les Ardoines à Vitry-sur-Seine
☎ 01 47 18 19 19
🖥 www.rollerparc.com

More leisurely routes can be found along the Promenade Plantée, allée de la Reine Marguerite in the Bois de Boulogne (on weekends), Quai de la Tournelle (on Sundays) and Canal St-Martin (from 12:00–18:00).

Ice-skating is possible throughout the year at the city's ice rink and at Disneyland (*see* opposite page), and in winter on place de l'Hôtel-de-Ville and in the Tuileries gardens.

Above: *Model boats for hire to sail on the Octagonal Basin in the Jardin des Tuileries.*
Opposite: *Disneyland Paris provides entertainment for the whole family.*

Alternative Paris
Cimetière des Chiens
(et Autres Animaux Exotiques)

The pet cemetery in Asnières is filled with the graves of a variety of pets including cats, dogs, rabbits and even horses.

The most famous pet buried here, however, must be the loveable canine film star, **Rin Tin Tin** (1918–1932). During World War I, an American, Lee Duncan, found a shell-shocked puppy in the French trenches. The dog was named Rin Tin Tin and was taken to America where he had an extremely successful career in the film industry. He was brought back to France after he died.

Fun for Children

Parisian society is driven by the wealthy and childfree. You see remarkably few small children around and few concessions are made for them. People are having families later and there is a tendency for Parisians to move to the suburbs when they start a family. That said, however, Paris has plenty to offer children, from parks and gardens (*see* page 40), to puppet shows, museums (*see* pages 37–39), and theme parks (*see* opposite panel).

Ice Rink
The Patinoire des Buttes-Chaumont
✉ 30 rue Édouard-Pailleron, 19th
☎ 01 42 08 72 20

Cimetière Des Chiens
✉ 4 pont de Clichy, Asnières-sur-Seine
🕐 10:00–18:00 Mar–Oct, 10:00–16:00 Tue–Sun Oct–Mar
Ⓜ Mairie de Clichy

FUN FOR CHILDREN

Disneyland Paris

A miniature version of its American parents but growing fast, Disneyland is visited by over 12.5 million people each year. Five themed areas cluster round the towering spires of **Sleeping Beauty's Castle**. Start early and you can get round everything in one day.

Vintage cars and horse-drawn carriages ply **Main Street, USA** – small town East Coast America c1900 – which is also the route of the daily grand parades (usually late afternoon). Don't buy all your souvenirs in this concentration of shops and eateries, as each area has its own themed merchandise. Above the main entrance is the first of four stations of the **Disneyland Railroad**, a little steam train that chugs round the edge of the park.

Frontierland is yee-ha Wild West, with a Mark Twain riverboat steamer, a ghostly mansion, shooting gallery, and the scream-making Big Thunder Mountain roller-coaster among the rides and attractions.

In **Adventureland** are the Temple of Doom rollercoaster, tree-top home of the Swiss Family Robinson, an adventure island complete with rope walkways, Pirates of the Caribbean and Aladdin's Cave.

The pastelled **Fantasyland**, home of Mickey, Pluto et al, is heartland of the Disney ideal and the best area for small children, with rides on Dumbo, giant teacups, ferris wheel, toy train and merry-go-round, and gentle cruises through the

---

Theme Parks

France Miniature

A giant map of France with waist-high miniatures of its monuments and villages.

✉ Elancourt
☎ 01 30 16 16 30
🖥 www.franceminiature.com
RER Line C to St-Quentin-en-Yvelines, then bus no. 411

Parc Astérix

Popular theme park based on the adventures of Astérix the Gaul.

✉ Plailly
☎ 03 44 62 34 34
🖥 www.parcasterix.fr
RER Line B3 to Aéroport Charles de Gaulle 1 station, then a shuttle bus.

Disneyland Paris

✉ Marne-la-Vallée
☎ 01 60 30 60 30; from UK: 0990-030 303
🖥 www.disneylandparis.com
RER Line A or TGV to Marne-la-Vallée-Chessy.

Opposite: *Musée
Carnavalet is a
treasure trove of
Parisian history*
Below: *Île St Louis is
an oasis of tranquil-
ity in the city centre.*

fairy tales, past the children of the world,
and the enchanting stories of Pinocchio,
Snow White and Peter Pan.

The park's newest attraction, **Walt
Disney Studios**, brings film, animation and
television production to life with a *Sunset
Boulevard* sound stage, a production back-
lot and animation studios.

Festival Disney provides themed evening entertainment, food and drink outside
the main park. There is also a spectacular
Buffalo Bill Wild West Show and barbecue
every evening.

Walking Tours

Paris is a city to be savoured slowly. Take
comfortable shoes, decide on an area, then
wander. Allow time to enjoy the flower
seller beside a tiny wrought-iron fountain,
the brightly canopied pavement café rich
with the smell of aniseed and fresh coffee, a
subtly carved stone doorway, the statuesque
mime artist perched on a concrete bollard. It
is almost impossible to get lost. If your feet
collapse under you, you will never be far
from a metro. And if you haven't seen all
the top 10 sights, it doesn't really matter.
They will still be there next time.

Île St Louis Walk (Map D–F4)
Start at metro Pont Marie. Cross the bridge and turn left onto Quai d'Anjou. Turn right past Square Barye, and right again onto Quai de Béthune. Take the first right, then first left onto Rue St Louis en Île. At Rue des Deux Ponts, turn left, then right onto Quai d'Orléans. Follow this round to the Pont St Louis, then turn right onto Rue St Louis en Île. Back at Rue des Deux Ponts, turn left for Pont Marie and the metro.

Marais Walk (*see* map D–F3 and page 24)
Start at metro St Paul. Go right along Rue St Antoine, past the Church of St Louis-St Paul and the Hôtel de Sully. Turn left up Rue de Birague into Place des Vosges. At the top of the square, turn left into Rue des Francs Bourgeois, right into Rue Sévigné, past the **Musée Carnavalet** (*see* page 37) and left into Rue du Parc Royal. To the right, on Rue Thorigny, is the **Musée Picasso** (*see* page 37). Go straight on. The road becomes Rue des 4 Fils. Turn left into Rue des Archives and left again, back onto Rue des Francs Bourgeois. Turn right on Rue Pavée and you will come out on Rue St Antoine, near the metro station.

Louvre and Surrounds Walk (*see* map D–D2)
Start at metro Palais-Royal and walk west along Rue de Rivoli. Turn right into Rue Castiglione, cross Place Vendôme and continue up Rue de la Paix to the Place de l'Opéra. Turn left along Boulevard des Capucines, which turns into Boulevard de la

> **St Louis**
> Born in 1214, King Louis IX succeeded to the throne at the age of 12. The years of regency under his mother led to rebellion among the feudal nobility, but once he had taken over the government Louis established legal and administrative reforms and promoted wider education. He fought in the Crusades, brought back many holy relics to France, and was responsible for the building of Sainte-Chapelle and the Sorbonne. Louis is revered for his sense of justice and his personal piety and religious devotion. He died in Tunis in 1270 from the plague.

Above: *The flamboyant Grand Palais was built for the 1900 Exposition.*

The Grand Parades
In 1810 a grand parade was held on the **Champs-Elysées** to mark the wedding of Napoleon and his second wife, Marie-Louise. In 1840 Napoleon's body was paraded here on its return from St Helena, and in 1871 the Germans marched to proclaim the end of the Franco-Prussian War. The French held victory parades here in 1919 and 1944, to mark the end of each World War. There are parades every Bastille Day (14 July) and Armistice Day (11 November); and it marks a key stage of the great cycling race, the Tour de France.

Madeleine, coming out beside the **Eglise de la Madeleine** (*see* page 35). Walk down into **Place de la Concorde** (*see* page 31), turn into the **Tuileries Gardens** (*see* page 40) and follow them back to the Louvre courtyard, and from there back to the metro.

Northwest Walk (*see* map D–D3)
Start in the **Place de la Concorde** (*see* page 31). Turn right, cross the Cours la Reine and down onto the quay. Walk past the houseboats to **Pont Alexandre III**. Climb up, take Av. Churchill, between the **Grand** and **Petit Palais** (*see* page 27) and turn left onto the **Champs-Elysées** (*see* page 27). At Rond Point, turn left onto Av. Montaigne and follow this to Place de l'Alma (with metro and Bâteau Mouche stops). Alternatively, take Av. George V back up to the Champs-Elysées and turn left for the Arc de Triomphe (*see* page 17), or right for the Place de la Concorde.

Les Invalides Walk (*see* map D–E4)
The lengthy Rue de l'Université runs from **St-Germain-des-Prés** (*see* page 34) to the **Eiffel Tower** (*see* page 14). As you move west, the feeling changes from the bustling, villagey atmosphere of the Left Bank to the sophisticated and self-contained emotions of the chic 7th arrondissement. Street life gives way to the closed porte-cocheres of the grand hotels, many of which are now ministries or embassies.

The residential Rue St Dominique, between the Invalides and the Champ de

Mars, is also a pleasant stroll with wonderful views of the Eiffel Tower. Small food shops are interspersed with those selling clothes, flowers and household goods, and it is a good hunting ground for *dégriffés* garments. Look out for the neoclassical Fontaine de Mars and, at no. 12, the wonderful Art-Nouveau Liceo Italiano. Just off it, the well-heeled clientèle of the charming Rue Cler market is reflected in the quality of the merchandise.

St-Germain-des-Prés Walk (*see* map D–E4)
From Place St-Germain-des-Prés (*see* page 32), walk down Rue Bonaparte, through Place St Sulpice, emerging on Rue de Vaugirard. Enter the **Jardins du Luxembourg** (*see* page 40); leave on the far side, on Boulevard St Michel. Turn left, then right onto Rue Soufflot for the **Panthéon** (*see* page 29). Walk back down Rue Soufflot. Halfway along, turn right onto Rue St Jacques. Turn left onto Rue des Écoles and right onto Rue de Cluny for the **Musée de Cluny** (*see* page 39); left for Boulevard St Germain. Cross and take Rue Boutebrie. At the top, turn left for Place St Michel and the metro.

> **Rivers of Sludge**
> Until Baron Haussmann got going in 1852, aided by the engineer Balgrand, Paris had only the most rudimentary drains and was renowned for the filth of its streets. Today, there are 2050km (1274 miles) of tunnel, nearly 6m (20ft) high and 4m (13ft) across, with 26,000 manholes. The Parisians are so proud of their sewers that since 1867 they have offered tours. Boat cruises were discontinued after someone used one in a successful bank robbery; now tours consist of a film, small museum and short walk.
> ✉ 93 quai d'Orsay, 7th
> **M** Alma-Marceau
> **RER** Pont de l'Alma

Below: *Hemingway and Sartre both drank in Les Deux Magots in St-Germain-des-Prés.*

Organized Tours
Bus Tours

The Paris Transport authority, **RATP**, offers several sightseeing options which often cost less than those offered by commercial operators. For more information contact RATP's Bureau de Tourisme (*see* side panel).

L'Open Tour offers open-deck bus tours along three circuits: central Paris 2¼hrs, Montmartre 1¼hrs, Bastille–Bercy 1hr. It is possible to hop on and off at more than 40 stops. Schedules vary.

There are also a number of private tour operators such as **Paris Vision** and **Cityrama**.

Boat Trips

A number of companies provide boat excursions (with English commentary available) on the Seine.

Bâteaux Mouches have the largest and best known of the sightseeing boats. They run tours every 30 minutes from 10:00–20:00 and every 20 mins from 20:00–23:00, summer; in low season, boats leave at 11:00, 14:30, 16:00 and 21:00 daily) from the Right Bank, Pont de l'Alma (**M** Alma Marceau). Commentaries are in French, German and English. They also offer lunch (13:00), and dinner cruises (20:30).

Bâteaux Parisiens have tours every 30-minutes (10:00–23:00) in summer; hourly (10:00–22:00) in winter, from Port de la Bourdonnais, Pont d'Iéna, 7th (**M** Bir Hakeim/Trocadéro) and Quai de Montebello, 5th (**M** Maubert-Mutualité/St-Michel). They also offer lunch (12:15) and dinner cruises (20:30).

Vedettes du Pont Neuf have trips every 30min (10:30–22:30 in summer, every 45

Bus Tours
RATP
✉ place de la Madeleine, 1st
☎ 08 36 68 77 14
💻 www.ratp.fr
M Madeleine

L'Open Tour
✉ 13 rue Auber, 9th
☎ 01 42 66 56 56
💻 www.paris-opentour.com
M Havre Caumartin or Opéra

Paris Vision
✉ 214 rue de Rivoli, 1st
☎ 01 42 60 30 01
M Tuileries

Cityrama
✉ 4 place des Pyramides, 1st
☎ 01 44 55 61 00
M Pyramides

Boat Trips
Bâteaux Mouches
☎ 01 42 25 96 10 (booking)
☎ 01 40 76 99 99 (info)
💻 www.bateaux-mouches.fr

Bâteaux Parisiens
☎ 01 44 11 33 44
💻 www.bateauxparisiens.com

Vedettes du Pont Neuf
☎ 01 46 33 98 38
💻 www.pontneuf.net

Batobus
☎ 01 44 11 33 99

Left: *A trip on a tour boat is an ideal way to view the city's sights.*

mins (10:30–22:00 winter), from the Square du Vert Galant, Île de la Cité (**M** Cité). Discounts for Paris Visite ticket holders.

Batobus has an unguided water bus every 25 minutes and stops at the Eiffel Tower, Musée d'Orsay, the Louvre, Notre Dame, Hôtel de Ville, Champs-Élysées and St-Germain-des-Prés. They only run from 10:00–19:00 Apr–Oct (to 21:00 Jun–Sep).

Canal Trips

The Parisian canals can also be explored with the help of a few tour operators. **Paris Canal** offer three-hour cruises on the Seine and Canal St-Martin (one per day each way, two on weekends and public holidays). **Canauxrama** offers a three-hour cruise on the Canal St-Martin (two departures each way daily).

Walking Tours

Paris Walking Tours offer the best walking tours of Paris in English which focus on a variety of themes. *Pariscope* and *L'Official des Spectacles* list a number of themed walks (in French).

Bicycle Tours

Several companies offer bicycle rental and guided tours (try **Paris à Vélo C'est Sympa**).

Canal Trips
Paris Canal
✉ Quai Anatole France, Musée d'Orsay and Parc de La Villette, 19–21 quai de la Loire, 19th
☎ 01 42 40 96 97
🖥 www. pariscanal.com
M Jaurès

Canauxrama
✉ Port de l'Arsenal, opp. 50 blvd de la Bastille, 12th
M Quai de la Rapée
✉ Bassin de la Villette, 13 quai de la Loire, 19th
☎ 01 42 39 15 00
M Jaurès
🖥 www. canauxrama.com

Walking Tours
Paris Walking Tours
☎ 01 48 09 21 40
🖥 www. paris-walks.com

Bicycle Tours
Paris à Velo c'est Sympa!
Guided cycle tours and bike hire.
✉ 22 rue Alphonse Baudin, 11th
☎ 01 48 87 60 01

Above: *Exclusive shops line the Place Vendôme.*

Shops

Paris is a shopaholic's fantasy land, with everything on offer from haute couture and haute cuisine. It's just a matter of looking in the right place.

HAUTE COUTURE
Triangle d'Or, 1st and 8th
(**M** *Franklin D Roosevelt or Alma Marceau*)

Av. Montaigne
Prada, 10;
Valentino, 17–19;
Christian Lacroix, 26;
Christian Dior, 30;
Max Mara, 31;
Celine, 36;
Louis Vuitton and Dolce & Gabbana, 22;
Nina Ricci, 39;
Thierry Mugler, 49;
Calvin Klein, 53.

Ave George V, 8th
Armani Collezione, 41;
Balenciaga, 10;
Givenchy, 3;
Jean-Paul Gaultier, 44.

Rue du Faubourg St-Honoré, 8th
(**M** *Madeleine or Concorde*)
Hermès, 24;
Chloe and Comme des Garçons, 54;
Lanvin, 15 and 22;
Prada, 6;
Versace, 62;
Yves St Laurent, 38.

Rue Cambon, 1st
(**M** *Madeleine*)
Chanel, 31;
Maria Luisa, 2;
Costume National, 5.

Rue St-Germain, 6th
(**M** *St-Germain-des-Prés*)
Onward, 147;
Paula Ka, 192;
Ramosport, 188;
Sonia Rykiel, 175;

Marais
Rue des Rosiers, Place des Vosges, Rue de Rivoli, Rue de Turenne and Rue des Francs Bourgeois have interesting shops.

Prêt-à-porter

Many famous couture houses have cheaper ready-to-wear showrooms on the Left Bank. Those after even greater bargains should look for *dégriffé* signs. These denote designer products with the original label cut out, which are sold off at vast discounts due to overproduction or slight shop soiling. Good hunting grounds include Rue St-Placid, Rue des Saints-Pères, Boulevard St-Michel, and Rue du Vieux Colombier. Rue Bonaparte is the shopping street of the Left Bank, but lock up your credit cards and window shop.

SHOPS

La Goutte d'Or, 18th

A collection of shops and stalls and a market on Mon, Wed, Sat.

DESIGNER VINTAGE & DISCOUNTS

Anna Lowe
✉ 104 rue du Faubourg St-Honoré, 8th,
☎ 01 42 66 11 32,
M Champs-Elysées-Clemenceau.

Annexe des Createurs
✉ 19 rue Godot de Mauroy, 9th,
☎ 01 42 65 46 40,
M Madeleine.

Le Mouton à Cinque Pattes
✉ 19 rue Grégoire-de-Tours, 6th,
☎ 01 43 29 73 56,
M Odéon.

DEPARTMENT STORES

La Samaritaine
✉ 19 rue de la Monnaie, 1st, ☎ 01 40 41 20 20, 🖥 www.lasamaritaine.com
M Pont Neuf.

Le Bon Marché
✉ 24 rue de Sèvres, 7th, ☎ 01 44 39 80 00, 🖥 www.bonmarche.fr
M Sèvres-Babylone.

Galeries Lafayette
✉ 40 bd Haussmann, 9th, ☎ 0142 82 30 25, 🖥 www.galerieslafayette.com
M Chaussée d'Antin/RER Auber.

Printemps
✉ 64 bd Haussmann, 9th, ☎ 01 42 82 50 00, 🖥 www.printemps.com
M Havre-Caumartin.

Bookshops

Bouquinistes
These book stalls have been here for hundreds of years. Antiquarian, new and second-hand in a variety of languages and on all subjects.
✉ along the Left Bank Quais, 5th
M St-Michel

Brentano's
✉ 37 av de l'Opéra, 2nd
☎ 01 42 61 52 50
M Opéra

Espace IGN
✉ 107 rue La Boétie, 8th
☎ 01 43 98 85 00
M Franklin D Roosevelt

Shakespeare & Co
✉ 37 rue de la Bûcherie, 5th
☎ 01 43 26 96 50
M St-Michel

WH Smith
✉ 248 rue de Rivoli, 1st
☎ 01 44 77 88 99
M Concorde

Tea and Tattered Pages
✉ 24 rue Mayet, 6th
☎ 01 40 65 94 35
M Duroc

Village Voice
✉ 6 rue Princesse, 6th
☎ 01 46 33 36 47
M Mabillon

Left: *La Samaritaine, opened in 1869, was the world's first department store.*

The Perfect Picnic
Poilâne
Possibly the best bakery in Paris. The speciality is a large country loaf that has become known everywhere as a poilâne.
✉ 8 rue du Cherche-Midi, 6th
Ⓜ Sèvres-Babylone/ St-Sulpice

Guillemard Traiteur
Delicatessen, pattiseries, ice cream and chocolate.
✉ 241 rue St-Jacques, 5th
RER Port Royale

Barthélémy
Cheese.
✉ 51 rue de Grenelle, 7th
Ⓜ Rue du Bac

Fauchon
Glorious food; absolutely everything; 13 branches across Paris.
✉ 30 place de la Madeleine, 8th
Ⓜ Madeleine

Below: *Shopping in the market – a great French tradition – is now sadly under attack from supermarkets.*

Markets

Paris has a thriving collection of markets, selling everything from food to fleas.

Rue Mouffetard

The most famous market in Paris, with beautiful displays of exotic shellfish, heaps of lemons, North African spices, Italian cheeses, Greek vine leaves, Chinese dried mushrooms, French strawberries, olives and cheeses, vats of *choucroute* and spits of roasting chickens.
⊕ *daily,*
Ⓜ *Monge, Censier Daubenton.*

Marché des Enfants-Rouges

The oldest covered market in Paris, founded in 1612, home to all sorts of affordable *charcuteries*, patisseries and lovely little specialist shops selling flowers and chocolate.
✉ *rue de Bretagne, 3rd,*
⊕ *09:00–20:00 Tue– Sat, 09:00–14:00 Sun,*
Ⓜ *Arts et Métiers.*

Rue de Buci

Less well-known but equally as atmospheric as rue Mouffetard. Go in the early evening when the street is crowded with locals shopping for their evening meal.
⊕ *daily,*
Ⓜ *St-Germain-des-Prés, Mabillon.*

Place du Tertre

Overflowing with a mass of pavement artists (licensed at two easels per square metre) and gawping tourists, it is still fun to look around here. The atmosphere bubbles, but most of the art is sadly third-rate, while the many cafés and restaurants are grossly overpriced.
✉ *next to Sacré*

Coeur, Montmartre,
M *Abbesses.*

Marché Edgar Quinet

One of the more exotic of the city's markets, this lively event at the foot of Tour Montparnasse is home to street traders, buskers and food vendors from across the globe. On Sundays there is a fine art exhibition.
✉ *bd Edgar Quinet,*
🕐 *07:00–14:30,*
Wed, Sun,
M *Edgar Quinet.*

Place Louis-Lépine

Tucked in behind the Conciergerie is Paris's most charming flower market. On Sundays it is given over to birds.
✉ *Île de la Cité, 4th,*
🕐 *daily; flowers Mon–Sat, birds Sun,*
M *Cité.*

Marché aux Timbres

A stamp-collector's haven.
✉ *Cour Marigny, 8th,*
🕐 *09:00–19:00 Thu, Sat and Sun,*

M *Champs-Élysées-Clemenceau.*

St-Ouen

Grand-daddy of all local flea markets, selling anything antique or merely secondhand, including clothes.
✉ *17 av de la Porte de Clignancourt,*
🕐 *09:00–19:00 Sat–Mon,*
M *Porte de Clignancourt.*

Porte de Vanves

Smaller and less touristy than the others and with a remote chance of a bargain.
✉ *Av Georges-Lafenestre and Av Marc-Sangier,*
🕐 *07:00–18:00 Sat, Sun,*
M *Porte de Vanves.*

Porte de Montreuil

Probably the most chaotic of the weekend flea markets this giant free-for-all has some treasures hidden among the dross.
✉ *Ave du Professeur André Lemière,*
🕐 *08:00–18:00 Sat–Mon,*
M *Porte de Montreuil.*

Above: *Traditional flower stalls are still to be found in this bustling modern city.*

Specialist Food Shops

A La Mère de la Famille
Superb chocolate since 1761.
✉ 35 rue du Faubourg-Montmartre, 9th
M Grands Boulevards

Café Verlet
Wonderfully aromatic coffee to drink here or take away, plus a wide range of dried and glacé fruits.
✉ 256 St-Honoré, 1st
M Pyramides

La Maison de la Truffe
Dedicated to the truffle, in all its gourmet variations.
✉ 19 place de la Madeleine, 8th
M Madeleine

Right: *Perhaps not the grandest in town, but the Ritz is the only hotel in Paris to have spawned songs and catchphrases.*

Youth Accommodation
Fédération Unie des Auberges de Jeunesse (HI)
Central Reservation office for all Hostelling International affiliates.
✉ 24 bd Jules Ferry 11th
☎ 01 43 57 02 60
📠 01 40 21 79 92
💻 www.fuaj.fr
🕐 daily 08:00–22:00
M République

HipHop Hostels
Excellent website with details of and connections to 8 of the best youth hostels in Paris.
💰 from 15 euros
💻 www.hiphop hostels.com

Hôtels des Jeunes (MIJE)
Three hostels in the Marais (4th; **M** St-Paul, Pont-Marie). All former aristocratic residences.
Le Fauconnier
✉ 11 rue du Fauconnier
☎ 01 42 74 23 45;
Le Fourcy
✉ 6 rue de Fourcy
☎ 01 42 74 23 45;
Maubisson
✉ 12 rue des Barres
☎ 01 42 74 23 45
Jean Monnet
☎ 01 43 13 17 00.

WHERE TO STAY

Paris accommodation covers every range, but little of it is cheap. Most places charge per room, not per person and include a continental breakfast. Because so many of the hotels are in older properties, rooms and beds are often small (certainly by American standards) and may only offer a shower, rather than a bath. Few cheaper properties have lifts. You should also check whether cheaper hotels take credit cards. Book ahead during peak seasons (spring and autumn).

There are accommodation booking offices at the main tourist office and the Gare de Lyon. Almost all major international chains have at least one hotel in the city. The vast French Accor Group, which includes the Formule, Novotel, Mercure, Ibis, Libertel and Sofitel chains, has dozens of properties in Paris at all levels of price and luxury, ☎ 01 60 77 27 27, 💻 www.accorhotels.com. Timhotel has 15 properties scattered throughout the most popular areas of the city; most are mid-sized, mid-range properties with a degree of charm and personal attention ☎ 01 44 15 81 15; 💻 www.timhotel.com

PALACE HOTELS

These few hotels are so famous and plushy they are tourist attractions in their own right. Very expensive.

Le Bristol Paris

(Map D–C2)

This intimate palace hotel offers exellent personalized service in luxurious surroundings. Opened In 1925, it recently underwent major renovations and now features a restaurant, fitness center, beauty and spa salon, swimming pool, garden and original art and Gobelin tapestries.

✉ 112 rue du Faubourg St-Honoré, 8th, ☎ 01 53 43 43 00,
📠 01 53 43 43 01,
🖳 lebristolparis.com
M Miromesnil.

Hôtel de Crillon

(Map D–D2)

Absolute luxury. The 104 rooms and 43 suites of this neo-classical palace have all been refurbished in Louis XV style. There is a fitness centre, boutique, and excellent dining options.

✉ 10 place de la Concorde, 8th,
☎ 01 44 71 15 00,
📠 01 44 71 15 02,
🖳 www.crillon.com
🖰 crillon@crillon.com
M Concorde.

Four Seasons George V (Map D–B2)

Offers everything to be expected from a luxurious palace hotel, such as large, elegantly furnished guest rooms, award-winning dining, a spa and health club.

✉ 31 av George V, 8th, ☎ 01 49 52 70 00,
📠 01 49 52 70 10,
🖳 www. fourseasons.com
🖰 paris@fourseasons. com
M George V.

Le Grand Inter-Continental

(Map D–D3)

Right beside Opéra Garnier, this vast – and vastly expensive – hotel is the chain's European flagship, recently renovated in the grand style.

✉ 2 rue Scribe, 2nd,
☎ 01 40 07 32 32,
📠 01 42 66 12 51,
🖳 www.

interconti.com
M Opéra

The Plaza Athenée

(Map D–C2)

A charming palace hotel that combines the most recent technology with its prestigious, classic French style.

✉ 25 av Montaigne, 8th, ☎ 01 53 67 66 65,
📠 01 53 67 66 66
🖳 www.plaza-athenee-paris.com
M Franklin D. Roosevelt.

The Ritz (Map D–D2)

Coco Chanel lived here, Hemingway called it paradise. Now owned by Mohammed el Fayed, the Ritz is still a byword of gilded luxury and elegance, perfectly situated in the heart of Paris.

✉ 15 place Vendôme, 1st,
☎ 01 43 16 30 30,
📠 01 43 16 36 68,
🖳 www.ritzparis.com
M Tuileries.

The Islands

A wonderful area – central yet peaceful and well situated for food, evening strolls and sightseeing.

LUXURY
Jeu de Paume
(Map D–F4)
A 17th-century *jeu de paume* (early tennis) court offers discreet luxury. No restaurant.
✉ *54 rue St-Louis en l'Île, 4th,*
☎ *01 43 26 14 18,*
📠 *01 40 46 02 76,*
💻 *www. jeudepaumehotel.com*
Ⓜ *Pont Marie.*

MID-RANGE
Deux Îles (Map D–F4)
A charmingly converted 17th-century mansion. Bed and breakfast only.
✉ *59 rue St Louis en l'Île, 4th,*
☎ *01 43 26 13 35,*
📠 *01 43 29 60 25,*
Ⓜ *Pont Marie.*

BUDGET
Henri IV (Map D–E4)
Very simple and very popular. Only four rooms have private baths.
✉ *25 place Dauphine, Île de la Cité, 1st,*
☎ *01 43 54 44 53,*
Ⓜ *Cité.*

Beaubourg, Les Halles, the Marais and Bastille

An excellent area with numerous small hotels – central, pleasant for strolling; filled with charming eateries.

LUXURY
Pavillon de la Reine
(Map D–F4)
Small, elegant courtyard mansion rebuilt to original plans in one of the city's most beautiful squares.
✉ *28 place des Vosges, 3rd,*
☎ *01 40 29 19 19,*
📠 *01 40 29 19 20,*
💻 *www.pavillon-de-la-reine.com*
Ⓜ *Chemin Vert, St-Paul.*

La Bretonnerie
(Map D–F3)
Small, comfortable 17th-century hotel. No restaurant.
✉ *22 rue Ste-Croix-de-la-Bretonnerie, 4th,*
☎ *01 48 87 77 63,*
📠 *01 42 77 26 78,*
💻 *www. Bretonnerie.com*
Ⓜ *Hôtel de Ville.*

MID-RANGE
St-Merry (Map D–E3)
17th-century presbytery and 19th-century brothel; stylishly converted; furnished with Gothic bric-à-brac.
✉ *78 rue de la Verrerie, 4th,*
☎ *01 42 78 14 15,*
📠 *01 40 29 06 82,*
💻 *www.hotelmarais. com*
Ⓜ *Hôtel de Ville.*

Castex (Map D–F4)
Charming, popular and recently refurbished.
✉ *5 rue Castex, 4th,*
☎ *01 42 72 31 52,*
📠 *01 42 72 57 91,*
💻 *www. castex-paris-hotel.com*
Ⓜ *Bastille.*

Montmartre and the Northeast

A little way out, but perfect for those on a moderate budget. Has vibrant nightlife; many cheap hotels, especially near the stations, some handling rough trade.

LUXURY
Terrass' Hôtel
(Map A–A2)
Charmingly decorated,

a good restaurant and excellent views.

✉ 12 rue Joseph-de-Maistre, 18th,
☎ 01 46 06 72 85,
📠 01 42 52 29 11,
🖥 www.terrass-hotel.com
M Blanche.

MID-RANGE
Villa Royale

(Map A–A3)
Not the most salubrious area, but this hotel in a historic building is a charming riot of colour with friendly service.

✉ 2 rue Duperré, 9th,
☎ 01 55 31 78 78,
📠 01 55 31 78 70,
🖥 royale@leshotelsdeparis.com
M Pigalle.

BUDGET
Prima Lépic

(Map A–A2)
Bright and airy town house hotel in the heart of Montmartre.

✉ 29 rue Lépic, 18th,
☎ 01 46 06 44 64,
📠 01 46 06 66 11,
M Blanche.

Hôtel du Marché

(Map D–F2)
Simple, comfortable,

slightly off the beaten track, but very cheap.

✉ 62 rue du Faubourg, St-Martin, 10th,
☎ 01 42 06 44 53,
M Château d'Eaul,
RER Gare du Nord.

The Louvre and Opéra

Convenient but uninspiring area. Excellent for shopping, lousy for nightlife, though the palace hotels near the Louvre create their own glamour.

LUXURY
Régina (Map D–D3)

Delightful Art-Deco building filled with antiques.

✉ 2 place des Pyramides, 1st,
☎ 01 42 60 31 10,
📠 01 40 15 95 16,
🖥 www.regina-hotel.com
M Pyramides.

MID-RANGE
Tuileries (Map D–E2)

A cosy hotel near the Tuileries gardens.

✉ 10 rue St-Hyacinthe, 1st,
☎ 01 42 61 04 17,
📠 01 49 27 91 56,
M Tuileries.

Gaillon-Opéra

(Map D–D3)
Warmly welcoming 19th-century building with wooden beams and flowery curtains.

✉ 9 rue Gaillon, 2nd,
☎ 01 47 42 47 74,
📠 01 47 42 01 23,
🖥 www.bestwestern.com
M Opéra.

Northwest Paris: The Rive Droite

Home to some of the finest hotels in Paris, dripping with money and celebrities. Nightlife centred on the Champs-Élysées. Not for tight budgets.

LUXURY
Balzac (Map D–B2)

Small, discreet, but extremely luxurious; excellent restaurant.

✉ 6 rue Balzac, 8th,
☎ 01 44 35 18 00,
📠 01 42 25 24 82,
M George V.

Hôtel Costes K

(Map D–B3)
Ultra-chic, ultra-modern boutique hotel with cool art and hip staff.

✉ 81 av Kleber, 16th,
☎ 01 44 05 75 75,
📠 01 44 05 74 74,
💻 costes.k@
wanadoo.fr
Ⓜ Trocadéro.

MID-RANGE
Résidence Lord Byron (Map D–C2)
Pleasant small courtyard hotel.
✉ 5 rue Châteaubriand, 8th,
☎ 01 43 59 89 98,
📠 01 42 89 46 04,
Ⓜ George V.

The Mayflower
(Map D–C2)
Pleasing hotel under same management as Résidence Lord Byron. No restaurant.
✉ 3 rue Châteaubriand, 8th,
☎ 01 45 62 57 46.
📠 01 42 56 32 38,
💻 mayflower@escapade-paris.com
Ⓜ George V.

The Eiffel Tower, Les Invalides and the Musée d'Orsay

Fairly quiet and sober, this area is splendidly central and the prices are considerably lower than across the river.

LUXURY
Duc de St-Simon
(Map D–D4)
Elegant, welcoming hotel with a small, flourishing garden. No restaurant.
✉ 14 rue de St-Simon, 7th,
☎ 01 44 39 20 20,
📠 01 45 48 68 25,
💻 duc.de.saint.simon@wanadoo.fr
Ⓜ Rue du Bac.

MID-RANGE
Le Pavillon
(Map D–C3)
Former convent; abundant charm; central courtyard; tiny rooms.
✉ 54 rue St-Dominique, 7th,
☎ 01 45 51 42 87,
📠 01 45 51 32 79,
Ⓜ La Tour Maubourg.

Thoumieux
(Map D–C3)
10 comfortable, but simply furnished rooms, attached to a lively bistro.
✉ 79 rue St-Dominique, 7th,
☎ 01 47 05 49 75,
01 47 05 36 96,

💻 www.thoumieux.com
Ⓜ La Tour Maubourg.

Rive Gauche and Montparnasse

Lively and entertaining area; numerous comfortable, middle-of-the-range hotels; wall-to-wall restaurants. An excellent place to stay.

LUXURY
L'Hôtel (Map D–E4)
Oscar Wilde died here in 1900. The hotel has come a long way since then. Beautiful furniture and a general air of extravagance. Renovated in 1968, each room has a story. Room 16 is a reconstruction of Oscar Wilde's; room 36 has Mistinguett's furniture.
✉ 13 rue des Beaux-Arts, 6th,
☎ 01 44 41 99 00,
📠 01 43 25 64 81,
💻 www.l-hotel.com
Ⓜ St-Germain-des-Prés.

Hôtel d'Angleterre
(Map D–D4)
Once the British Embassy, later Hem-

ingway's home, the treaty which ended the American War of Independence was prepared in this 18th-century building, although it was signed further up the street, as Franklin refused to set foot on British soil. Charming, comfortable and peaceful hotel surrounds small flower-filled courtyard.
✉ 44 rue Jacob, 6th,
☎ 01 42 60 34 72,
📠 01 42 60 16 93,
Ⓜ St-Germain-des-Prés.

MID-RANGE
Ste-Beuve
(Map D–D5)
This small hotel successfully mingles cool, understated elegance and a cosy, welcoming atmosphere.
✉ 9 rue Ste-Beuve, 6th, ☎ 01 45 48 20 07,
📠 01 45 48 67 52,
🖥 www.paris-hotel-charme.com
Ⓜ Vavin.

Welcome Hotel
(Map D–E4)
Warm, friendly hotel on a lively street; overlooks flower market.
✉ 66 rue de Seine, 6th, ☎ 01 46 34 24 80,
📠 01 40 46 81 59,
🖥 www.welcomehotel-paris.com
Ⓜ Odéon.

Esmeralda
(Map D–E4)
Small 16th-century hotel with charmingly eccentric décor.
✉ 4 rue St-Julien-le-Pauvre, 5th,
☎ 01 43 54 19 20,
📠 01 40 51 00 68,
Ⓜ St-Michel.

The Île de France
Disneyland Paris
(Map F–B1)
Six huge theme hotels and a self-catering complex on site. All prices available.
✉ Marne-la-Vallée/Chessy,
☎ 01 60 30 60 30 or UK 0870 503 0303,
🖥 www.disneylandparis.com

Le Versailles
(Map G–B1)
Friendly hotel near château; spacious rooms; pretty terrace; reasonable prices.
✉ 7 rue Saint-Anne, Versailles,
☎ 01 39 50 64 65,
📠 01 39 02 37 85,
🖥 www.hotel-le-versailles.fr
Ⓜ Odéon.

Accommodation Bureaux
Alcôve et Agapes
(Map E–C3)
Singles and doubles bed and breakfast from 50–120 euros.
✉ 8 bis rue Coysevox, 18th,
☎ 01 44 85 06 05,
📠 01 44 85 06 14,
🖥 www.bed-and-breakfast-in-paris.com
✉ info@bed-and-breakfast-in-paris.com

France Lodge Locations (Map D–C1)
Non-profit organisation arranges accommodation in private homes and apartments from about 25 euros pp per night. Plus a range of longer-stay holiday apartments.
✉ 2 Rue Meissonier, 17th,
☎ 01 56 33 85 85,
📠 01 56 33 85 89,
🖥 www.paris-rental.com
Ⓜ Wagram.

Haute Cuisine
Talleyrand's chef, Marie-Antoine Carême (1784–1833), revived a sumptuous pre-Revolutionary tradition of French court cuisine, rich with cream and cognac, foie gras and truffles, and published a seminal work, *L'Art de la Cuisine Française*. Fifty years later, another great Parisian, Escoffier (1846–1935), was hailed as 'King of Chefs and the Chef of Kings'. The reputation of French cuisine was assured.

The grand tradition continued into the 1980s and the short-lived vogue for *nouvelle cuisine* (minute portions, beautifully arranged). Since then, fashion has moved on to the *cuisine du terroir*, as chefs recreate the classic recipes with healthier, less fatty ingredients, revive an interest in French regional food, and even begin to incorporate foreign ideas, brought back by an increasing number of French tourists.

EATING OUT

Parisians appear obsessed by food. The city is a gastronome's heaven, the spiritual and physical home of haute cuisine, with possibly the greatest concentration of fine food in the world. However, all is not as rosy as it might seem in paradise.

The State of the Art

French eating habits are changing. Most women now work and simply do not have the time to cook long, luscious meals; busy, cholesterol-aware office workers are shunning the traditional three-course lunch in favour of a quick snack at their desk; and supermarkets are squeezing out many smaller shops.

Everyday food is much simpler than before, with frozen and vacuum-packed ingredients common and a booming trade in ready-prepared meals. These are usually traditional dishes such as *cassoulet* or *coq au vin*, but there is a new vogue for chilli con carne and lemon meringue pie.

All this change, tragically, has begun to filter through into the restaurants and cafés and you can no longer be assured of quality. There are still delightful traditional restaurants and chic new bistros with talented and imaginative young chefs. But there are also many corner-cutting brasseries serving dull, unimaginative, microwaved food, who rely on a flashy shopfront and gullible passing tourists to fill their tills.

What to Eat
The Internal Clock

A typical French **breakfast** is milky coffee or hot chocolate with a croissant or baguette and jam. Many hotels, used to international visitors, may add the choice of ham and cheese, fruit juice and yoghurt.

Lunch can be a simple snack or a full meal. Go early, as restaurants begin to fill up from 12:00 onwards. If on a limited budget, consider eating your main meal at midday as the fixed price lunch menus are excellent value, while a light snack, such as an omelette and salad, can be horribly expensive. Some places, however, also do a good-value one-course *plat du jour*.

Alternatively, the best option is to **picnic**. The key ingredients – bread, paté, cheese, sausage and fruit – are all easily available, as are bottled water, wine and cans of soda. Many delicatessens also sell ready-made salads, quiches, made-up sandwiches and pizza. Some parts of the parks are off limits, but there are plenty of benches and fountain steps, and the quays beside the Seine are excellent picnic spots.

Dinner begins surprisingly early, at about 19:00. Do not arrive much after 21:00 because most places will then be full. Ideally, it is safer to reserve in advance. Eating after the theatre or opera is not easy, unless you go 'ethnic' or to the more bohemian areas of the Left Bank. Again, most restaurants have a range of two- or three-course set menus at different prices, all of which are cheaper than the à la carte options. Some also include wine and coffee.

Above: *France produces over 400 cheeses, labelling the best with a certificate of origin similar to the AOC of fine wine.*
Opposite: *Heaped snails drenched in garlic butter – a great French tradition.*

Le Sandwich

French bread is designed to be bought daily and eaten the same day. The various sizes and weights are all government-controlled.

The *baguette* (a long stick-like loaf) is the most common bread in France. If it is too much, you can also buy a *demi* (half) or a *ficelle* (a smaller thinner stick). The *bâtard* is the same weight as a baguette but shorter and fatter. For sandwiches, you may like to look at the heavier, crusty round *pain de campagne*, either brown or white.

Right: *Cafés have been a central part of social and intellectual life in Paris since the 17th century, providing meeting places for artists and intelligentsia alike. Many of these cafés retain their original interior, and still play a prominent role in everyday life.*

Where to Eat
Bistro or Brasserie

Paris has more restaurants per head than any other city in the world. Choosing where to eat can be one of the greatest pleasures of your holiday (*see pages 65–69* for a small sampling of all the wonderful options). A few top restaurants are so famous that you have to book months in advance, and probably take out a large bank loan. For a good, relatively cheap meal, select an area, then wander the side streets, reading menu boards outside until you find one that makes you salivate. Avoid those with too long a menu. Food is likely to be fresher and cooked specially for you with only a limited number of dishes on offer. The 1st arrondissement, just behind the Louvre, has many excellent options at a higher price. For cheaper meals, the best hunting areas are Montmartre/Pigalle and the Latin Quarter.

The café/bar serves drinks, coffee and light snacks such as *croque-monsieur* (toasted ham and cheese sandwich) or *assiette*

Just Desserts

Most cheaper French restaurants have a very standard list of desserts. They will almost certainly include *tarte au pomme* (apple tart or other fruit tart), *mousse au chocolat*, *îles flottantes* (light meringue on a sea of custard), and *crème caramele*. Other common possibilities include ice creams and sorbets, profiteroles, and *tarte tatin* (upside down, caramelized apple pie).

anglaise (assortment of salamis and cold meats) all day. It is always cheaper to stand at the bar than to sit at a table and it may be even more expensive to sit at one of the premium pavement tables.

The **brasserie** originally started life as a beerhouse but has grown over the years into another form of eatery. Brasseries serve a basic menu of simple food such as *steak frites* (steak and chips), shellfish, omelettes, sausage *andouillette* (tripe sausage) and *choucroute garnie* (sauerkraut with meats) – and, of course, different beers. They serve food all day and usually have a reasonably priced set meal to keep you going.

The '**bistro**' was named in 1917 by Russian emigrés (the word is Russian for 'quick'). Bistros began life as the Parisian fast-food joints, small, cheap and cheerful restaurants serving a limited menu of hearty, unpretentious food. In their present form, they are still small and cheerful, with a slightly more ambitious menu and wine list and, usually, with a bar attached.

As well as the individual restaurants, travellers on a moderate budget should take a look at some of the chains of brasseries, such as **Hippopotamus** and the more upmarket **Flo** chain; **Léon le Bruxelles**; Bistro Romain; and **Bistrot d' à Côté** chain, which are cheaper eateries managed by some of the city's great chefs.

> **Over Coffee**
> Café society flourished in 18th-century Paris. The cafés were places to meet friends, drink coffee and discuss politics or literature. Perhaps the most famous of them all was the **Café Procope** at no. 13 rue de l'Ancienne-Comédie. Here the *philosophes* would gather to debate at leisure. Voltaire was a frequent visitor and it is said that Diderot and d'Alembert first thought up the idea for their Encyclopedia here.

Below: *Take the weight off your feet, sip a drink and simply watch the world go by at a pavement café.*

Lie of the land
The French are nothing if not traditional. At a time when the New World is producing **wines** in steel vats, with plastic corks and labels stuffed with information on the grape varietals and helpful hints on how to serve them, the French cling to time-honoured methods of production and labelling. The name of the château and the AOC (area) take precedence over the possible taste of the wine. Which means that you need to know your Beaujolais from your Burgundy if you are to choose a suitable wine. If in doubt, ask the waiter for a suggestion.

Ethnic Options

Most of the cheaper French restaurants tend to have remarkably similar menus. However, the city is also home to an amazing array of other ethnic cuisines, brought here by Russian and Polish refugees, immigrants from Greece and Italy, and former colonials from North Africa, the Caribbean and Vietnam. Alongside these establishments are Thai, Japanese and Indian restaurants and even English and Irish pubs. Many of these are excellent, offer extraordinarily good value, are one of few viable options for vegetarians and can be a welcome change from another steak *au poivre*.

What to Drink

France is the world's greatest producer of wine, but the French nurse their glass of beer (lager-style) or Pernod, while wine is always accompanied by food, even if it is only a few canapés or petits fours.

On the whole, wine lists concentrate heavily on local vintages. Paris does sell wines from across France, but puts a very steep mark-up on famous names. As an affordable alternative, most eateries have excellent house wines, sold by the carafe or demi-carafe.

Right: *France may have competition, but still produces some of the world's finest wines.*

The Islands

La Charlotte en Île

One of the lovely *salons de thé* (tea-rooms) on this street.
✉ *rue St Louis en l'Île 24, 4th,*
☎ *01 43 54 25 83,*
🕐 *12:00–20:00, Thu–Sun,*
Ⓜ *Pont Marie.*

Les Fous de l'Île

Friendly; good value lunch; à la carte dinner.
✉ *33 rue des Deux Ponts, 4th,*
☎ *01 43 25 76 67,*
🕐 *12:00–23:00 Tue–Fri, from 15:00 on Sat, 12:00–19:00 Sun,*
Ⓜ *Pont Marie.*

Le Vieux Bistro

Traditional French cooking; warm and friendly. Moderate.
✉ *14 rue du Cloître Notre Dame, 4th,*
☎ *01 43 54 18 95,*
Ⓜ *Cité or St-Michel.*

Brasserie de l'Île St Louis

Well-established, relaxed brasserie specializing in food from Alsace. Moderate.
✉ *55 quai de Bourbon, 4th,*
☎ *01 43 54 02 59,*
Ⓜ *Pont Marie.*

Berthillon

Said to produce the best ice cream in France (also sold in nearby cafés).
✉ *31 rue St Louis en l'Île, 4th,*
☎ *01 43 54 31 61,*
Ⓜ *Pont Marie.*

Beaubourg, Les Halles, the Marais and Bastille

Au Pied de Cochon

A huge Paris institution. Originally served hearty fare to market workers; now the place to come for breakfast after a heavy night out. Moderate.
✉ *6 rue Coquillière, 1st,*
☎ *01 40 13 77 00,*
🕐 *24 hours,*
Ⓜ *Les Halles.*

Bofinger

Seafood specialist; delightful Art Nouveau décor. Moderate.
✉ *5–7 rue de la Bastille, 4th,*

Above: *The vast majority of France's beers are light, gassy lagers, although there are a few darker still beers, some of the strongest brewed by monks.*

It's a Bit Fishy

When reading menus, one of the most difficult things is deciphering the seafood section. A few of the most common seafood options include: *crevettes* (prawns); *langoustine* (crayfish); *moules* (mussels); *homard* (lobster); *coquilles* (scallop); *calmar* (squid); and *pieuvre* (octopus). Among the white fish, you are likely to meet *merlue* or *colin* (hake); *morue* or *cabillaud* (cod); *sole* (sole); *églefin* (haddock); *rouget* (red mullet); *flétan* (halibut); *St Pierre* (John Dory); and *saumon* (salmon).

☎ 01 42 72 87 82,
M Bastille.

Chicago Meatpackers

Ribs and T-bones for homesick Americans.
☒ 8 rue Coquillière, 1st,
☎ 01 40 28 02 33,
M Les Halles.

Jo Goldenberg

The most famous Jewish deli and restaurant in Paris.
☒ 7 rue des Rosiers, 4th,
☎ 01 48 87 20 16,
M St-Paul.

L'Ambassade d'Auvergne

Lunch and dinners for the really hungry. Sausages and hams of this region are among the best in France.
☒ 22 rue du Grenier St-Lazare, 3rd,
☎ 01 42 72 31 22,
M Rambuteau.

L'Ambroisie

Magnificent Michelin 3-star restaurant, in a superb setting. Book one month ahead. Very expensive.

☒ 9 place des Vosges, 4th,
☎ 01 42 78 51 45,
M St-Paul, Chemin Vert.

Le Trumilou

Authentic menu from the early 20th century.
☒ 84 quai de l'Hôtel de Ville, 4th,
☎ 01 42 77 63 98,
⏲ lunch and dinner, until 23:00 Mon–Sat and until 22:30 Sun,
M Hôtel de Ville.

Montmartre and the Northeast

Le Perroquet Vert

A charming traditional bistro, close to Montmartre, with a roaring log fire in winter, beamed roof, check tablecloths, and traditional country cuisine.
☒ 7 rue Cavalotti, 18th,
☎ 01 45 22 49 16,
⏲ closed Sat and Mon lunch and all day Sun; from 1–19 Aug,
M Abbesses or Anvers.

Brasserie Wepler

Try the seafood at this 100-year-old brasserie. Moderate.

☒ 14 place de Clichy, 18th,
☎ 01 45 22 53 24,
M Place Clichy.

Chez Haynes

One of the first American restaurants, with a jazz theme and soul food. Cheap.
☒ 3 rue Clauzel, 9th,
☎ 01 48 78 40 63,
M St-Georges.

Macis et Muscade

Excellent example of a restaurant du quartier (neighbourhood restaurant). Impeccable service.
☒ 110 rue Legendre, 17th,
☎ 01 42 26 62 26,
⏲ lunch Sun, Tue–Fri, dinner until 22:30 or 23:00 Tue–Thu, Fri, Sat,
M La Fourche.

Thu Thu

Good, cheap Vietnamese cooking, with a good choice of vegetarian dishes and an ultra-cheap lunch menu.
☒ 51 bis rue Hermel, 18th,
☎ 01 42 54 70 30,
⏲ closed Sun lunch

and Mon,
M *Simplon.*

The Louvre and Opéra

This area has several palace hotels with superb dining rooms, among them the Ritz, Inter-Continental, and the Bristol (*see page 55*).

Le Grand Véfour

On the edge of the Jardin du Palais Royal; frequented by the Paris elite since 1784. Lunch and dinners.
✉ *17 rue de Beaujolais, 1st,*
☎ *01 42 96 56 27,*
🕐 *until 22:15, Mon–Fri,*
M *Pyramides.*

Angelina's

Ultimate chic, a gilded 19th-century tearoom. Expensive.
✉ *228 rue de Rivoli, 1st,*
☎ *01 42 60 82 00,*
M *Tuileries.*

Chartier

A barn set up in 1892 to feed workers cheaply. Still offers good, cheap food, appalling service and spectacular Belle Epoque décor.
✉ *7 rue du Faubourg-Montmartre, 9th,*
☎ *01 47 70 86 29,*
M *Rue-Montmartre.*

La Mousson

Traditional Khmer (Cambodian) food well cooked; extremely reasonable prices.
✉ *9 rue Térèse, 1st,*
☎ *01 42 60 59 46,*
🕐 *Mon–Sat lunch and dinner, closed Aug,*
M *Pyramides.*

Joe Allen

Friendly American restaurant-bar; great atmosphere; excellent brunch. Also serves lunch and dinner.
✉ *40 rue Pierre Lescot, 1st,*
☎ *01 42 36 70 13,*
🕐 *12:00–16:00, Sat and Sun,*
M *Étienne Marcel.*

Le Grand Colbert

A charming, classic brasserie, popular with the theatrical crowd. Expensive.
✉ *2–4 rue Vivienne, 2nd,*
☎ *01 42 86 87 88,*
🕐 *late,*
M *Bourse.*

Willi's Wine Bar

English-run wine bar; pleasant décor, good wine and interesting menu. Moderate.
✉ *13 rue des Petits-Champs, 1st,*
☎ *01 42 61 05 09,*
M *Bourse.*

Northwest Paris: The Rive Droite

This is the home of haute cuisine with a cluster of superb, vastly expensive restaurants, including Chiberta, Laurent, Ledoyen, Taillevent, and palace hotel dining rooms, among them the Crillon, George V and Plaza Athénée (*see page 55*).

Chicago Pizza Pie Factory

American pizzas and razmatazz. Moderate.
✉ *5 rue de Berri, 8th,*
☎ *01 45 62 50 23,*
M *George V.*

Fauchon

There are several eateries, from café to self-service to grand restaurant in this vast temple to food. Try the menu, then buy the ingredients. All price ranges.

✉ 30 place de la Madeleine, 8th,

☎ 01 47 42 90 10,

Ⓜ Madeleine.

L'Avenue

Art Deco restaurant; Provençale-inspired food, popular with fashion gurus. Moderate to expensive.

✉ 41 av Montaigne, 8th,

☎ 01 40 70 14 91,

Ⓜ Alma Marceau.

La Maison d'Alsace

Huge, bright and busy brasserie, specializing in Alsatian food.

✉ 39 av des Champs-Élysées, 8th,

☎ 01 53 93 97 00,

Ⓜ Franklin D. Roosevelt.

Lucas Carton

Belle-époque décor; superbly innovative cuisine; 3 Michelin stars. Book ahead. Very expensive.

✉ 9 place de la Madeleine, 8th,

☎ 01 42 65 22 90,

Ⓜ Madeleine.

Maxim's

A Paris institution, the building is a national monument. Superb cuisine; sophisticated live music. Book ahead. Very expensive.

✉ 3 rue Royale, 8th,

☎ 01 42 65 27 94,

Ⓜ Concorde.

Eiffel Tower, Les Invalides, St-Germain and Musée d'Orsay

Jules Verne

Highest restaurant in Paris; very popular. Book way ahead. Seamless service; excellent traditional food. Expensive.

✉ 2nd floor of the Eiffel Tower, 7th,

☎ 01 45 55 61 44,

Ⓜ Bir-Hakeim.

Casa Corsa

Delicious Corsican cuisine; simple; sophisticated; moderate.

✉ 25 rue Mazarine, 6th,

☎ 01 44 07 38 98,

🕐 lunch Tue–Sat, dinner until midnight Mon–Sat,

Ⓜ Odéon.

À la Cour de Rohan

A peaceful tearoom with delicious deserts.

✉ 59–61 rue St-André des Arts, 6th,

☎ 01 43 25 79 67,

🕐 12:00–19:30 daily, 12:00–00:00 Fri and Sat, Apr–Oct,

Ⓜ Mabillon.

Guen Maï

Cozy vegetarian restaurant serves organic daily specials.

✉ 6 rue Cardinale, 6th,

☎ 01 43 26 03 24,

🕐 11:45–15:30 Mon–Sat,

Ⓜ St-Germain-des-Prés or Mabillon.

Thoumieux

A jolly bistro with hearty, country-style cuisine. Cheap.

✉ 79 rue St-Dominique, 7th,

☎ 01 47 05 49 75,

Ⓜ Invalides.

Rive Gauche and Montparnasse

A foodie's mecca offering everything from the sublime to the hamburger. For cheap, cheerful places, stroll the streets behind St-Julien le Pauvre or between Place St-André-des-Arts and St-Germain-des-Prés.

Brasserie Lipp

Famous brasserie; clientèle has included the rich and famous, from Hemingway to Madonna. The 1920s décor is a national monument. Moderate.
✉ 151 boulevard St-Germain, 6th,
☎ 01 45 48 53 91,
Ⓜ St-Germain-des-Prés.

Le Café des Délices

A delightful little place south of the Jardins de Luxembourg. African-Asian décor; delicious, reasonably priced Mediterranean food; novelty munchies for those with a sweet tooth.
✉ 87 rue d'Assas, 6th,
☎ 01 43 54 70 00,
🕐 closed Aug,
Ⓜ Vavin.

La Coupole

Huge brasserie; one of the great artists' hangouts of the 1920s and 30s; bustling ever since.
✉ 102 boulevard du Montparnasse, 14th,
☎ 01 43 20 14 20,
Ⓜ Vavin.

Le Kitch

Mediterranean-inspired food; colourful and kitsch décor.
✉ 10 rue Oberkampf, 11th,
☎ 01 40 21 94 14,
🕐 lunch Mon–Fri, dinner until 02:00 daily,
Ⓜ Filles du Calvaire.

Le Bistrot du Dôme

Charming, popular seafood restaurant; menu changes daily.
✉ 2 rue de la Bastille, 4th,
☎ 01 48 04 88 44,
🕐 lunch and dinner until 23:30 daily,
Ⓜ Bastille.

Le Procope

Founded in 1686, this is one of the oldest and most famous cafés in Paris. During the Revolution it became the Café de Zoppi and the drinking haunt of Marat. Voltaire, Balzac and Verlaine were other habitués. Today visitors come to see the portrait of Dr Guillotin. Traditional food; moderate.
✉ 13 rue de l'Ancienne Comédie, 6th,
☎ 01 40 46 79 00,
Ⓜ Odéon.

La Tour d'Argent

One of the meccas of French gastronomy since 1582. The traditional French food is about the best you will ever taste – the duck even comes with a certificate. Book way ahead. Very expensive.
✉ 15-17 quai de la Tournelle, 5th,
☎ 01 43 54 23 31,
Ⓜ Maubert-Mutualité.

Perraudin

Traditional bistro serving onion soup and boeuf bourguignon to local students. Cheap.
✉ 157 rue St-Jacques, 5th,
☎ 01 46 33 15 75.

Above: Parisian streets are not particularly child-friendly, but there are occasional treats.

ENTERTAINMENT

Paris has an extraordinary range of entertainment and nightlife from the sublime to the decidedly sleazy. Listings of latest events can be found in *l'Officiel des Spectacles* and *Pariscope* (six-page English supplements), both available weekly on Wednesdays from any newsagent.

Kiosque Théâtre sell theatre tickets at half price (plus commission) on the day of any play, musical, concert, opera or ballet.

Fnac has an excellent online and telephone booking service with credit card operated pick-up points in all their stores, and handles everything from theatre to rock and sporting events.

Virgin Megastore also has an excellent ticket counter and online and telephone service, while www.fr.lastminute.com has a good array of cheap seats.

Painting the Town Red

The best known red-light district in the city is in **Pigalle**, at the foot of Montmartre, centred on the famous **Moulin Rouge**. The area is increasingly sleazy, with touts pulling people through the neon-flashing doors into a variety of clubs, some trendy, others decidedly dodgy. The surrounding streets support a bevy of prostitutes in various stages of undress. Single women should avoid the area after dark.

Kiosque Théâtre
Has two outlets:
⊠ 15 place de la Madeleine, 8th
M Madeleine
⊠ parvis Montparnasse, 15th
M Montparnasse Bienvenüe

Virgin Megastore
⊠ 52–60 av des Champs-Élysées, 8th
☎ 08 25 02 30 24
🖳 www.virginmega.fr
M Franklin D. Roosevelt

Fnac Forum des Halle
⊠ Les Halles
☎ 08 92 68 36 22
🖳 www.fnac.com
M Les Halles

Music

Astonishingly, in spite of the superb **Conservatoire de Paris** and **Opéra**, Paris had little influence on music until the mid-19th century, mainly producing only frothy entertainment, with some honourable exceptions such as Lully and Gluck, both of whom were foreign. Parisian Berlioz was forced to work abroad.

As with the other arts, Parisian music reached its zenith in the 19th century when composers such as Rossini, Chopin, Liszt, Wagner, Offenbach, César Franck, Saint-Saëns, Fauré, Debussy and Ravel flocked into the city, along with Diaghilev's Russian ballet.

At the same time popular nightlife was becoming increasingly important. Possibly the city's greatest home-grown contribution has been to **cabaret**, sparked by the glamorous, high-kicking chorus line of the **cancan** (1830, to music by Offenbach), eventually producing singers such as Maurice Chevalier and Edith Piaf, and showcasing the great American Josephine Baker and German Marlene Dietrich.

There is always music available – on the streets, in the churches and museums, cafés, clubs and concert halls. Classical concerts (sometimes free) held in several churches, including Notre Dame, Eglise du Val-de-Grâce, St-Julien-le-Pauvre and St-Eustache, museums including the Musée d'Art Moderne, the Musée de l'Homme and in numerous parks. Look out for handbills or see listings.

Cité de la Musique
✉ 221 av. Jean Jaurès, 19th
☎ 01 44 84 44 84
💻 www.cite-musique.fr
Ⓜ Porte de Pantin

Salle Pleyel
✉ 252 rue du Faubourg St-Honoré, 8th
☎ 01 45 61 53 01
💻 www.cite-musique.fr
Ⓜ Terne
🕐 Reopening in 2004/5 after restoration.

Maison de Radio France
✉ 116 av. du Président Kennedy, 16th
☎ 01 42 20 42 20
💻 www.radiofrance.fr
Ⓜ Passy, RER Kennedy Radio France

Below: *The ornate façade of Opéra Garnier is a mixture of baroque and classical, with statuary and medallions relating to the arts and music.*

Opéra Bastille
✉ 2–6 place de la
Bastille, 12th
Box office: ✉ 130 rue
de Lyon
☎ 08 92 89 90 90
🖥 www.
opera-de-paris.fr
🕐 11:00–18:30
Mon–Sat
M Bastille

Opéra Garnier
✉ Place de l'Opéra,
9th
☎ 08 92 89 90 90
🖥 www.
opera-de-paris.fr
M Opéra
RER line A Auber

Comédie Française
✉ 2 rue de Richelieu,
1st
☎ 01 44 58 15 15
🖥 www.
comedie-francaise.fr
M Palais-Royal

The **Cité de la Musique** has music and dance schools, a theatre, concerts, the Musée de la Musique and a summer classical music festival.

Opera and Ballet
The magnificently elaborate **Opéra Garnier** (*see* page 22) is still home to opera, but is more commonly used for classical ballet these days. The Opéra National company has moved across to the fortress-like **Opéra Bastille**, built to commemorate the bicentenary of the storming of the Bastille prison in 1789.

Theatre
For French-speakers, there are numerous theatres, from the traditional to small experimental performance spaces.

The Comédie-Française
France's first national theatre, the Comédie-Française, has the official title of Le Théâtre Française.

It was founded in 1680 by Louis XIV and brought together two Paris theatre companies, the Hôtel de Bourgogne (itself an amalgamation of the Théâtre du Marais with Molière's own company, the Illustre Théâtre) and the Théâtre Guénégaud.

With a royal grant the company enjoyed a number of privileges, but they were abolished during the Revolution and the theatre disbanded.

Below: *The fortress-like Opera Bastille, adds a further dimension to the city's cultural facilities.*

Later re-established, it was granted a decree by Napoleon in 1812. The company has performed the works of all the great French dramatists, notably the plays of Corneille, Molière and Racine.

Above: *As elsewhere, Imax films have become popular in Paris*

Cinema

Since Auguste and Louis Lumière opened the world's first cinema in Paris in 1895, the city has remained the centre of a small but steady French film industry that has produced several of the world's finest filmmakers, including Jean Renoir (son of the painter), Abel Gance, Marcel Pagnol, Jean Cocteau, Jacques Tati, François Truffaut, Jean-Luc Goddard and Louis Malle, and some of the world's favourite stars, such as Maurice Chevalier, Charles Boyer, Jean-Paul Belmondo, Simone Signoret, Brigitte Bardot, Jeanne Moreau, Gérard Dépardieu, Catherine Deneuve and Alain Delon.

There are huge numbers of cinemas throughout the city, showing everything from Hollywood blockbusters to retrospectives and art films. VO (Version Originale) means it's sub-titled; VF (Version Française) means it's been dubbed.

Cinema With a Difference

Within **Parc de la Villette** (*see* page 21) are a number of entertaining attractions. The **Géode** is a massive geodesic sphere made of 6500 stainless steel triangles, with a 1000m² (10,750 sq ft) hemispherical cinema screen.

<u>Géode</u>
✉ Cité des Sciences, av Corentin-Cariou, 19th
☎ 08 92 68 45 40
🖥 www.lageode.fr
🕐 10:30–21:30 Tue–Sun (until 19:30 Sun)
🚌 English-version headsets free from Geode information
M Porte de la Villette

<u>Cinaxe</u>
✉ Cité des Sciences
🕐 every 15 mins 11:00–13.00 and 14:00–17:00, Tue–Sun
See above for details.

<u>Louis-Lumière Cinema</u>
🕐 11:00, 11:30, 12:00, then every 30 mins from 14:00–17:30, Tue–Sun
Also:18:00 and 18:30 Sun and school holidays

Above: *The Millennium fireworks were such a success they repeat them every year.*

The **Cinaxe** moves and shakes the entire cinema as you watch. The **Louis-Lumière Cinema** shows the world's first movies. Elsewhere, the **Forum des Images** has around 6500 movies with images of Paris, viewable on TVs and compact screens. The city's official film museum, the **Cinemathèque Française**, is in the Palais de Chaillot, with a viewing screen in the Grands Boulevards.

Forum des Images
✉ Forum des Halles, Porte Saint-Eustache, 1st
☎ 01 44 76 63 00
🕐 12:00–21:00 Tue–Sun

Cinemathèque Française
✉ Palais de Chaillot
Ⓜ Trocadéro
Viewing screen:
✉ 42 Boulevard de Bonne Nouvelle, 10th
Ⓜ Bonne Nouvelle
☎ 01 56 26 01 01
(for both)

Festival d'Automne
☎ 01 53 45 17 00
🖥 www. festival-automne.com
🕐 mid-Sep to Dec

Festivals

The Parisians are capable of making a festival of almost anything. Check the listings in magazines (*see* page 70) or www.paris.org for details of what is on at any given moment.

Big events to look out for are the **Banlieue Bleues** (five weeks of jazz, gospel, R&B etc. in St-Denis, Mar–Apr); the **Paris Jazz Festival** (free open-air concerts, May–Jul); **Le Cinema en Plein Air** (Parc de la Villette, Jul–Aug); **Paris-Plage** (the city quais are turned into beaches; mid-July to mid-Aug); **Les Journées du Patrimoine** (all sorts of buildings, which are normally closed to the public, fling open their doors; third weekend in Sep); and the **Festival d'Automne** (cutting-edge theatre, dance and music).

Bastille Day (14 July) is celebrated with dancing in the place de la Bastille. **New Year** is celebrated along the Champs-Elysées, with midnight fireworks at the Eiffel Tower and a procession on New Year's Day.

Nightclubs

There are clubs for all from 70s revival to S&M. Most have tight security and you will probably have to persuade the bouncers to let you in. Avoid trainers, look cool and talk English – it helps. To be French, do several clubs a night, starting with the DJ bars and going on to the real thing at about 02:00, when Londoners would be heading home to bed.

Cabaret

There are many Parisian cabaret theatres (mostly in the Montmartre area). Traditional revues with chorus girls in feathers; gay and drag acts; sex shows; comedy and acid political satire (good French needed). Famous venues are fun, but very expensive.

Moulin Rouge

The famous Doriss Girls together with stunning costumes, feathers and sequins.

✉ *82 bd de Clichy, 9th,*
☎ *01 53 09 82 82,*
🖥 *www. moulinrouge.fr*
M *Blanche.*

Crazy Horse

Offers a live show every evening.
✉ *12 av George V, 8th,*
☎ *01 47 23 32 32,*
🖥 *www. lecrazyhorseparis.com*
M *George V.*

Lido de Paris

Spectacular shows enhanced by the latest special effects.
✉ *116bis, av des Champs-Élysées, 8th*

Stringfellows
Topless dancers, shiny poles and plentiful alcohol.
✉ 22 av. des Ternes
☎ 01 47 66 45 00
M Ternes

Studio 287
A huge venue specializing in the Ibiza sound.
✉ 33 av de la Porte d'Aubervilliers, 18th
☎ 01 48 34 00 00

Rex
The Paris home of electronic music.
✉ 5 bd Poissonnière, 2nd
☎ 01 42 36 10 96
M Bonne Nouvelle

Below: *The Moulin Rouge has been famous for its Parisian nightlife since the 1890s.*

Maurice Chevalier
The entertainer Maurice Chevalier (1889–1972) was born at Ménilmontant, near Paris, and through a long career in show business as actor and singer became for many the archetypal Frenchman. He first appeared on stage as a singer at the age of 17 and three years later was starring as dancing partner of the famous Mistinguett at the Folies-Bergère. As the film industry grew so he became a star of the screen. He gave a memorable performance with Hermione Gingold in the film *Gigi*, set in late 19th-century Paris, in which the elderly couple recalled the gaiety of their youth.

Below: *The quaint charm of Au Lapin Agile belies its reputation as a hotbed of satirical cabaret.*

☎ *01 40 76 56 10,*
🖥 *www.lido.fr*
M *George V.*

Folies-Bergère
Have been offering shows for 130 years. Now perform a techno French cancan.
✉ *32 rue Richer, 9th,*
☎ *01 44 79 98 98,*
🖥 *www. foliesbergere.com*
M *Cadet, Grands Boulevards.*

Au Lapin Agile
Satirical cabaret. Music, singing, comedy and poetry.
✉ *22 rue Saules, 18th,*
☎ *01 46 06 85 87,*
🖥 *www. au-lapin-agile.com*
M *Lamarck Caulaincourt.*

Le Zèbre
Chanson and satire in a restored art-deco cinema.
✉ *63 bd de Belleville, 20th,*
☎ *01 43 55 55 55,*
M *Père Lachaise*

Spectator Sports
Cycling
After a gruelling tour of France and neighbouring countries, the Tour de France arrives back in Paris in July. To have a go yourself, *see page 49.*
☎ *01 41 33 15 00,*
🖥 *www.letour.fr*

Tennis
Tennis is popular in France – which is why they produce so many good professionals. The French Tennis Open is one of the Grand Slam tournaments, held at the beginning of June.
✉ *Stade Roland Garros, 2 av Gordon-Bennett, 16th,*
☎ *01 47 43 48 00,*
🖥 *www.french open.org*
M *Porte d'Auteuil.*

Running

All those joggers put their early morning exercise to good use in early April for the Paris Marathon.

✉ Champs-Elysées to av. Foch,
☎ 01 41 33 15 68,
💻 www.paris-marathon.com
M Charles-de-Gaulle-Etoile.

Rugby

Rugby is rapidly growing in popularity in France with a strong national league and a national team that is a strong contender for the Six Nations' Cup, played from mid-Feb to mid-April each year. The sport is governed by the Fédération Française de Rugby.

✉ 9 rue de Liège, 9th,
☎ 01.53.21.15.15,
💻 www.ffr.fr
M Liège.

Rugby and Football

In view of France's international strength, astonishingly Paris has only one top division team, Paris St-Germain. International matches are played at the Stade de France.

✉ Parcs des Princes, 24 rue du Commandant-Guilbaud, 16th,
☎ 01 42 30 03 60,
💻 www.psg.fr
M Porte d'Auteuil.
✉ Stade de France, rue Francis Pressensé, St-Denis,
☎ 08 92 70 09 00,
💻 www.stadedefrance.fr

Above: The Tour de France traditionally finishes on the Champs-Elysées.

Watching the Horses

Showjumping
World-class showjumping in March.
✉ Palais Omnisports, 8 bd Bercy, 12th
☎ 01 46 91 57 57
M Bercy

Steeple-chasing
In mid-May, the Prix du Président de la République brings in the international jetset for one of the world's premiere jump races.
✉ Hipodrome d'Auteuil, Bois de Boulogne
M Porte d'Auteuil

Flat-racing
In mid-June, the horsey crowd move to Chantilly for the Prix de Diane Hermès, the country's premier flat race.
✉ Chantilly
☎ 03 44 62 41 00
💻 www.paris-turf.com
RER Chantilly, 30 mins from Gare du Nord

Above: *The house that toppled a dynasty – Louis XIV nearly bankrupted France to build Versailles, a monumental folly that led directly to the French Revolution.*

<u>Château de Versailles</u>
Location: Map G
Distance from Paris: 20km (12 miles)
🖳 www.chateauversailles.fr/en/
🕐 Château: 09:00–18:30 May–Sep, 09:00–17:30 Oct–Apr; Tue–Sun, except public holidays. Arrive early to beat the tour buses; plan carefully as different sections are open at different times.
🚌 audio-guides and organized tours
💰 different prices for different sections
RER Line C5 to Versailles-Rive Gauche

<u>Tourist Office</u>
✉ 2 bis av de Paris
☎ 01 39 24 88 88
🖳 mairie-versailles.fr
🕐 09:00–19:00 Tue–Sun May–Sep, 10:00–18:00 Mon.

EXCURSIONS
The Suburbs

The suburbs have an odd mixture of styles and seem rather unplanned, with 50-year-old villas next to soulless apartment blocks. **La Défense** is ultra-modern, **Neuilly** is elegant, **St-Denis** surrounds a great medieval basilica, while American-style houses squat round the palace in **Versailles**. Generally, the more elegant suburbs are to the west, the poorer areas to the east, although the advent of Disneyland Paris with its new facilities and excellent transport has shifted the balance.

Château de Versailles

Until 1661, Versailles was a simple hunting lodge. Louis XIV, however, believed himself to be little short of divine and wanted a palace to match. It took 21 years for Le Vau and Hardouin-Mansart to complete a palace whose sheer size, with its long façade, leaves you gasping, although it was stripped of its furniture during the Revolution and many rooms are still very bare.

Louis XIII's original lodge is just visible at the back of the **Cour de Marbre**, totally engulfed by the enormous wings. In the north wing are the **Opéra Royal**, the **Chapelle Royale** (1710), and the **Grands Appartements**. The Salon d'Apollon was the throne room; the Salon de Mercure, the state bedroom; the Salon de Diane a games room; and the Salon de Mars a ballroom. The most magnificent is the **Galerie des Glaces** (Hall of Mirrors), its 17 windows arranged so that sunlight would reflect off mirrors and back outside, to make it seem as if the Sun King really shone. It was here that Bismarck made the Kaiser head of a united Germany, and Germany signed the Treaty of Versailles.

From 1727, Louis XV and Jacques-Ange Gabriel, began to create the **Petits Cabinets** which became the apartments of his mistress, Madame du Barry. In 1738 he moved from the state bedroom into the **Appartements du Roi**. The **Appartements de la Reine**, designed for Marie Leczinska in 1729, were in the south wing. They are now furnished as they would have been for Marie-Antoinette.

The magnificent **gardens**, restored to Le Nôtre's original 17th-century splendour, are vast. In front of the château is a terrace of lawns, fountains and pathways, studded by magnificent statues. Beyond this, stretch the Grand and Petit Canals.

To the right is the **Grand Trianon**. The first pavilion here was a trysting place where Louis XIV could meet his mistress. The current building became a private court. Carefully restored, it is now the most lavishly decorated of all the palace suites.

Between 1745 and 1749 Louis XV had the New Menagerie (a glamorous farmyard) built on the **Pavillon Français** for another royal mistress, Madame de Pompadour. In 1761 botanical gardens were laid out, though later changed to the English style preferred by Marie-Antoinette.

The **Petit Trianon** is an almost perfect little palace. Louis XVI gave it to his wife, Marie-Antoinette who spent her happiest moments here. She remodelled the gardens into artificial countryside and built a model village and farmhouse. The queen was near here when the Revolutionary mob attacked the palace.

The Sun King
Louis XIV (1638–1715) came to the throne in 1643, aged five, with his mother, Anne of Austria, as regent, but only took power after the death of Cardinal Mazarin in 1661.
In 1660 he married Infanta Maria Theresa of Spain. He spent 38 years at war with Spain, the Netherlands, Alsace, southern Germany and Italy while his Chief Minister, Colbert, enforced endless laws, creating a total dictatorship. Above all, Louis is remembered as the flamboyant 'Sun King' who thought himself divine, identified with Apollo, created a glittering era of lavish spending and great art, and bled the country dry.

Below: *The site of Versailles was originally marshland; 30,000 workers had to level and drain the area.*

Bois de Boulogne
Location: Map E–B3
Distance from Paris:
just outside the old city
gates, within metropol-
itan Paris.
☎ 01 42 15 00 11
📠 01 42 15 03 52
🖥 www.relais-bois-de-
boulogne.fr
✆ info@relais-bois-de-
boulogne.fr
🕐 not safe at night
M Porte Maillot, Porte
Dauphine, Porte
d'Auteuil, Sablons

Bois de Boulogne

Covering a massive 845ha (2085 acres), the Bois de Boulogne was a hunting preserve before it was enclosed in 1558 as a royal park. It became highly fashionable as a promenade and duelling ground when Louis XV opened it to the public, but it was only in 1852 that Baron Haussmann created a fully fledged public park after Napoleon III gave the area to the city. The Bois was inspired by London's Hyde Park, with its winding walks. There are several distinct areas. The children's **Jardin d'Acclimation** has a playground, petting zoo, miniature railway, giant doll's house, bowling alley and an art gallery and Internet workshop, the **Musée en Herbe**. The **Musée National des Arts et Traditions Populaires**, next door, has a fine rural crafts collection. The **Pré Catalan**, named after a 12th-century Pro-vençal minstrel murdered there, has a mag-nificent copper beech while the **Jardin de Shakespeare** is made up of plants men-tioned in his plays. There are also two large boating lakes and particularly fine formal gardens in the **Jardin des Serres d'Auteuil** and the **Parc de Bagatelle**, which surrounds a delightful house built in 64 days in 1775 as a bet between Marie-Antoinette and the Comte d'Artois.

The most famous of the many amateur and profes-sional sporting facilities are the **Roland Garros ten-nis stadium**, home of the French Open, and **Long-champs** (flat) and **Auteuil** (jump) racecourses.

Below: *The Bois de Boulogne offers an area of rural beauty and relaxation with-in a short distance of the centre of Paris.*

Left: *The Grande Arche de la Défense.*

La Grande Arche
Location: Map E–B3
Distance from Paris:
5km (3 miles)
✉ 1 parvis de la
Défense
☎ 01 49 07 27 57
🖳 www.grandearche.
com
🕘 09:00–19:00 sum-
mer, 09:00–18:00 winter
M Grande Arche de la
Défense
RER line A La Défense
exit: La Grande Arche

La Défense

A huge rebuilding programme planned to revitalize the inner suburbs, has taken place since the 1960s. The centre-piece, the **Grande Arche de La Défense** is a gleaming white 100m (330ft) cube. It was designed by Danish architect, Johann-Otto von Sprekelsen and inaugurated in 1989 to celebrate the Bicentennial of the Revolution. The sculptural canopy of 'clouds' is the work of British engineer Peter Rice. The views from the top are excellent. The multimedia information centre in the base of the arch has a wealth of information relating to Europe and the European Union.

A small museum at the **Info-Défense** tourist office (15 place de la Défense) has an interesting display of architectural plans, models and projects regarding the development of La Défense.

Defense of Paris
La Défense is named after the 1870–71 defence of Paris. Work began on this ultra-modern business park, the largest construction project since the Maginot Line, in 1955. Designed to preserve the city centre from over-development, it has become a vast, soulless open esplan-ade, surrounded by tower blocks. Many were considered revolu-tionary in their day. Sadly, all too many now look tired, although some of the buildings and many of the scattered sculp-tures, by artists such as Miró and Calder, are interesting. About 35,000 people live here, and 130,000 work in its many offices.

Above: *Surrounded by forest, Fontaine-bleau is one of France's most charming châteaux.*

Fontainebleau

Fontainebleau
Location: Map E–F6
Distance from Paris: 65km (40 miles) south-east of Paris
☎ 01 60 71 50 70
📠 01 60 71 50 71
🖳 www.musee-chateau-fontainebleau.fr
📧 chateau-de-fontainebleau@culture.fr
🕐 09:30–17:00 Oct–May, 09:30–18:00 Jun–Sep
M SNCF from Gare de Lyon to Fontainebleau-Avon, then bus

Louis the Fat (1108–37) first declared this area a royal hunting preserve and a vast and exceptionally beautiful forest still surrounds the town. In 1527, however, François I demolished the old fortress and commissioned the architect Gilles le Breton to build him the delightful Renaissance château which is the prime attraction. A favourite palace for generations of rulers, almost every future monarch added, demolished and altered bits of it. During the Revolution, it was stripped bare, the canal was drained and the fish were sold to the masses. Nevertheless, it is one of the most charming palaces in France, with a real sense of history and continuity. Napoleon loved Fontainebleau and spent much of his time here. He signed his abdication on 6 April 1814 in the dramatically named Cour des Adieux. The **Musée Napoléonien d'Art et d'Histoire Militaire** concentrates on his daily life.

Chartres

Like Notre Dame, the magnificent cathedral at Chartres stands on ground sacred to many religions over thousands of years. The earliest Christian church was built in the 4th century. It became a major pilgrimage centre in 876 when Charlemagne's grandson, Charles the Bald, presented the Sancta Camisia, supposedly the cloth worn by Mary while giving birth to Christ.

The crypt of the existing cathedral dates to 1024, while the spectacular Gothic church, soaring above the little town, was built in the early 13th century. Above all, it has 172 peerless 13th-century stained-glass windows, telling stories of heroes and the Bible, showing the lives of peasants and princes, honouring God, the saints and the people who paid for them in a unique record of medieval life and thought. Even the local merchants donated 42 windows, each showing the speciality of the guild.

The narrow streets around the cathedral have many delightful half-timbered buildings, several other fine churches and a Musée des Beaux-Arts.

Chartres
Location: Map E–A6
Distance from Paris: 88km (55 miles) southwest of Paris (SNCF from Gare Montparnasse to Chartres)
🖳 www.chartres.com
M Chartres Station from Paris Gare Montparnasse

Tourist Office
✉ Place de la Cathédrale
☎ 02 37 18 26 26
📠 02 37 21 51 91
✉ chartres.tourism@ wanadoo.fr

Chartres Cathedral
✉ Place de la Cathédrale
🕐 08:30–19:30 daily (1 Nov–Easter); 08:00–20:00 daily (Easter–1 Nov)
🚌 tours in English by world expert Malcolm Miller (☎ 02 37 28 15 58).

Left: *The beautiful cathedral of Chartres is justly famed for its fine stained-glass windows, especially for the clear 'Chartres blue' colour.*

Above: *Pont Alexandre III, named after the Russian Czar, was built for the Paris Exhibition in 1900.*

Tourist Offices
Paris
Information, hotel and entertainment bookings, transport, museum passes, bureau de change. ⊠ 25-27 rue des Pyramides, 9th ☎ 08 92 68 30 30 🖥 www. paris-touristoffice.com 🕐 High season: daily, 09:00–20:00. Low season: Mon–Sat, 09:00–20:00; Sun and holidays, 11:00–18:00. **M** Pyramides
Paris Ile-de-France
⊠ Carrousel du Louvre, 99 rue de Rivoli ☎ 08 26 16 66 66 🖥 www.paris-ile-de-france.com

---

French Tourist Offices Abroad
Australia: ⊠ 25 Bligh St, Level 20, Sydney, ☎ 02 9231 5244, 📠 02 9221 8682, 🕐 info.au@franceguide.com
Canada: ⊠ 1981 Avenue McGill College, Ste 490, Montreal, Quebec H3A 2W9, ☎ (514) 288 4264, 📠 (514) 845 4868, 🕐 canada@franceguide.com
Ireland: ⊠ 10 Suffolk St, Dublin 2, ☎ (01) 560 235 235, 📠 (01) 679 0814, 🕐 info.ie@franceguide.com
South Africa: ⊠ Oxford Manor, 1st floor, 196 Oxford Rd, Ilovo, 2196, ☎ (011) 880 8062, 📠 (011) 770 1666, 🕐 mdfsa@frenchdoor.co.za
UK: ⊠ 178 Piccadilly, London W1J 9AL, ☎ (09068) 244 123 (60p/min at all times), 📠 (020) 7493 6594, 🕐 info.uk@franceguide.com
USA: ⊠ 444 Madison Ave, 16th flr, New York, NY10020, ☎ (410) 286 8310, 📠 (212) 838 7855, 🕐 info.us@franceguide.com
Also offices in Miami, Beverley Hills and Chicago.

Getting There
By Air:
Flights to Paris from almost every country in the world. Direct scheduled services from many UK regional airports.

Airports:
Roissy-Charles de Gaulle, 30km (19 miles) northeast of Paris on autoroute A1. 24hr flight information and other advice in English, ☎ 01 48 62 22 80, 🖥 www.adp.fr
Airport transfers: RER line B3, every 8–15min.
Air France coaches (☎ 08 92 35 08 20) every 15–20min to

Place Charles de Gaulle-Etoile, Gare de Lyon, Monparnasse and Porte Maillot. RATP Roissybus (☎ 01 49 25 61 87) services every 15min to Opéra-Garnier. Journey time approximately 1hr.

Orly, 20km (12 miles) south of Paris on autoroute A6. 24hr flight information, ☎ 01 49 75 15 15. Airport transfers: RER Line B4 with connecting Orlyval shuttle at Antony; Line C with connecting shuttle bus or Orlyrail from Pont de Rungis. Air France coaches (☎ 08 92 68 77 14) depart every 12min to Les Invalides and Gare Montparnasse; The RATP Orlybus (☎ 08 92 68 77 14) leaves Denfer-Rochereau every 15 mins. The journey takes approximately 35min.

By Train:
Six main SNCF stations handle train services from all over France and also from most European countries.

All are served by metro and RER. For enquiries regarding the SNCF's mainline timetables, ☎ 08 92 35 35 35; for information and reservations for suburban services in English ☎ 08 36 68 77 14, 🖥 www.sncf.fr

Paris-Nord, ✉ 15 rue de Dunkerque, 10th. Eurostar services through the Channel Tunnel and some UK boat trains.

Paris-Saint-Lazare, ✉ Rue St-Lazare, 8th. UK boat trains.

Paris-Est, ✉ 10 place du 11 novembre 1918, 10th.

Paris-Montparnasse, ✉ 17 blvd de Vaugirard, 15th.

Paris-Austerlitz, ✉ blvd de l'Hôpital, 13th.

Paris-Gare de Lyon, ✉ place Louis Armand, 12th.

Eurostar, ☎ (UK) 08705 186 186, (France) 08 92 35 35 39, 🖥 www.eurostar.com

Documents

EU, other European, US, Canadian and New Zealand citizens will

Getting Around

Paris has an excellent pubic transport network – made up of the metro and buses, both run by **RATP** ☎ 08 36 68 77 14, 🖥 www.ratp.fr and the RER and suburban mainline rail services, run by **SNCF** ☎ 08 36 35 35 35, 🖥 www.sncf.fr Use the same tickets on all transport. Paris is divided into 8 concentric zones; clip more tickets if travelling further. Single tickets are expensive, a carnet of 10 offers a hefty discount. Cheaper still are the various passes such as the 1-day Formule 1, the 1-, 3- or 5-day Paris Visite (which also offers discounts on attractions, and the (Mon–Sun) or monthly (from 1st month) Carte Orange (ID and passport photo required). All tickets are available from main metro, RER and SNCF stations, while some passes are available at *tabacs*, tourist offices and airports. Metro stations are plentiful and trains run every couple of minutes between 05:30 and 01:00. Lines are numbered and colour coded on maps, but are named according to the last stop on the line. To change lines, trace the route to the last stop in the right direction and follow the Correspondance sign. There are good bus services during the day, but they stop or tail off after 20:30 and on Sundays.

need to have a current **passport**. Other nationals may require a **visa** and should therefore check with their nearest French embassy before departure. Drivers from Europe, North America, Australia and New Zealand can use their national driver's licence; others need an international licence. A green card is required for all foreign vehicles.

When to go

Any time of year. The climate is probably best and Paris looks prettiest in May/June and September/October. These are prime tourist times and also the festival seasons. Always make your hotel bookings in advance. Avoid travelling on the last weekends in July and August, the beginning and end of the French school holidays. In August Parisians go to the country, and many of the smaller shops and hotels close,

but the town is pleasantly empty.

Communications

Post

Stamps from La Poste offices, ☉ 08:00–19:00 Mon–Fri, 08:00–12:00 Sat. Post boxes are small, wall-mounted and yellow. The main post office, ✉ 52 rue du Louvre, 1st, ☎ 01 40 28 76 00, **M** Sentier, Les Halles, ☉ 24hr; for telephones and collecting poste restante mail.

Telephone

Most public telephones use stored value phone cards (available from *tabacs*, tourist shops, etc.). For cheap rate prepaid international calls with a coded card, ask for a *télécarte à puce*. Most boxes handle international calls and have multilingual instructions. Post offices and many cafés have pay phones (for local calls only). It is possible to use many national charge cards and GSM mobile phones (US

travellers will require tri-band phones). To phone Paris from abroad, dial the particular country's international access code (often 00 or use +) followed by the international country code for France (33), and then omit the 0, dialling the number 1 and the eight following digits. So to call Paris 01 22 44 66 88 from London, you would dial: 00 33 1 22 44 66 88.

Emergencies

EU Emergency: ☎ 112.
Police: ☎ 17.
Fire: ☎ 18.
SAMU (ambulance): ☎ 15.
Emergency doctor: ☎ 01 43 37 77 77.
Emergency dentist: ☎ 01 43 37 51 00 or 01 42 61 12 00.
Lost Property Office: ✉ 36 rue des Morillons, 15th, ☎ 08 21 00 25 25, **M** Convention.

Health

EU citizens are entitled to subsidized (not free) treatment. Fill in Form

E111 (from DSS offices) before travelling. You will have to pay, then claim for reimbursement. Full travel insurance is advisable. France is safe and clean, the water is drinkable and no vaccinations are needed. Pharmacists can often treat minor ailments.

Pharmacie des Champs, ✉ Galerie des Champs, 84 av des Champs-Elysées, 8th, ☎ 01 45 62 02 41, ⏰ 24hr, daily.

English hospitals:
Hertford British Hospital, ✉ 3 rue Barbès, 92300 Levallois-Perret, ☎ 01 46 39 22 22. M Anatole-France **American Hospital**, ✉ 63 boulevard Victor Hugo, 92202 Neuilly-sur-Seine, ☎ 01 46 41 25 25, M Porte-Maillot. Both private and expensive; most public hospitals have some English-speaking staff.

Insurance

A good travel insurance policy should cover all medical costs, including repatriation; the loss, theft or damage of any belongings and money; cancellation and delay; and third party damages should you cause an accident. Available from any reputable travel agent.

Safety

Paris is no more or less dangerous than any other major city. There are no real 'no-go' areas, although women should think twice about walking around the Gare du Nord/Pigalle area on their own at night. Otherwise, be sensible. Be careful crossing the roads – the traffic can be lethal. Don't carry all your money and valuables around with you; most hotels can provide a secure lock-up. Men should make sure their wallet is securely anchored in an inside pocket and women should use a handbag with a cross-shoulder strap and zip.

Further Reading

• Gilles Desmons, *Walking Paris*, New Holland Publishers, London, 1994. Walks in and around the city.
• Anne and Alain Riou (annual), *Paris Pas Cher, Editions du Seuil, Paris*. Excellent guide to bargains (theatre tickets to couturier gowns). French.
• *Guide Gault Millau Paris* (annual). The city's top food and drink listings, crammed with useful information. French.
• Robert Cole, *A Traveller's History of Paris*, Windrush, London, 1999. History of Paris.
• John Ardagh, *France in the New Century: Portrait of a Changing Society*: Introduction to modern-day France, its politics, its people and their idiosyncrasies.
• Ian Littlewood, *Paris: A Literary Companion*, John Murray, London, 1987. Writings on the city.
• Raymond Rudorff, *Belle Epoque: Paris in the Nineties*, Hamish Hamilton, London, 1972. Gay Paris at the turn of the century.
• Victor Hugo, *Les Misérables*, Penguin Classics. Social injustice, revolution and a rousing story.
• George Orwell, *Down and Out in London and Paris*, Penguin, London. Street life during the 1930s depression.
• Novels by Honoré de Balzac, Emile Zola and Simone de Beauvoir (English translation through Penguin Classics).

National Holidays
New Year's Day
• 1 January
Easter Sunday and
Monday
May Day • 1 May
VE Day • 8 May
Ascension Day
Whit Monday
(Pentecost)
Bastille Day • 14 July
Assumption Day
• 15 August
All Saint's Day
• 1 November
Armistice Day
• 11 November
Christmas Day
• 25 December

Useful Websites
French art and culture:
🖥 www.culture.fr
Event bookings:
🖥 www.fnac.com
Weather forecast:
🖥 www.meteo.fr/temps
French yellow pages:
🖥 www.pagesjaunes.fr
Information:
🖥 www.paris.org-good
Tourist office:
🖥 www.
paristouristoffice.com
Events:
🖥 www.timeout.com.
Transport:
🖥 www.eurostar.com
🖥 www.sncf.fr
🖥 www.ratp.fr
🖥 www.
britishairways.com
🖥 www.airfrance.fr
🖥 www.eurolines.com
🖥 www.batobus.com

Late at night keep to
well-lit streets. If in
doubt take a taxi.

French Embassies Abroad

Australia: ✉ 6 Perth
Ave, Yarralumla,
Canberra ACT 2600,
☎ (06) 62 16 01 00,
📠 (06) 62 16 01 27,
🖥 www.
ambafrance-au.org

Canada:
✉ 42 Promenade
Sussex, Ottawa
Ontario K1M 2C9,
☎ (613) 789 1795,
📠 (613) 562 3735,
🖥 www.
ambafrance-ca.org

Ireland:
✉ 36 Ailesbury Road,
Ballsbridge, Dublin 4,
☎ (01) 277 5000,
📠 (01) 277 5001,
🖥 www.
ambafrance-ie.org

New Zealand:
✉ Rural Bank
Building, 13th floor,
34–42 Manners Street,
Wellington,
☎ (04) 384 2555,
📠 (04) 384 2577,
🖥 www.
ambafrance-nz.org

South Africa:
✉ (Feb–Mar) 78
Queen Victoria Street,
Cape Town, 8001,
☎ (021) 422 1338;
📠 (021) 426 1996;
✉ (Apr–Jan) 250 Melk
St, New Muckleneuk
Pretoria 0181, ☎ (012)
425 1600, 📠 (012)
425 1609, 🖥 www.
ambafrance-rsa.org

UK:
✉ 58 Knightsbridge,
London SW1X 7JT,
☎ (020) 7073 1000,
📠 (020) 7073 1042,
🖥 www.
ambafrance-uk.org

USA:
✉ 4101 Reservoir
Road, NW, Washing-
ton DC 20007,
☎ (202) 944 6000,
📠 (202) 944 6166,
🖥 http://
ambafrance-us.org

Embassies and Consulates in Paris

Australia: ✉ 4 rue
Jean Rey, 15th,
☎ 01 40 59 33 00,
🖥 www.austgov.fr
M Bir Hakeim.

Canada: ✉ 35 av
Montaigne, 8th,
☎ 01 44 43 29 00,
🖥 www.amb-canada.fr
M Franklin D.
Roosevelt.

Ireland: ✉ 4 rue Rude, 16th, ☎ 01 44 17 67 00, **M** Argentine.
New Zealand: ✉ 7ter rue Léonard-da-Vinci, 16th, ☎ 01 45 01 43 43, 🖥 www.nzembassy.com/home.cfm?c=6 **M** Victor Hugo.
South Africa: ✉ 59 quai d'Orsay, 9th, ☎ 01 53 59 23 23, 🖥 www.afriquesud.net **M** Invalides.
UK: ✉ 35 rue Faubourg St-Honoré, 8th, ☎ 01 44 51 31 00, 🖥 www.amb-grandebretagne.fr **M** Concorde.
Consulate: ✉ 18 bis rue d'Anjou, 8th, ☎ 01.44.51.31.00, **M** Concorde, ⊕ 09:30–12:30 and 14:30–17:00.
USA: Embassy: ✉ 2 av. Gabriel, 8th, ☎ 01 43 12 22 22, 🖥 www.amb-usa.fr **M** Concorde.
Consulate: ✉ 2 rue St-Florentin, 1st, ☎ 08.10.26.46.26 (premium rate), **M** Concorde.

Money Matters

The currency is the euro, divided into 100 cents (called centimes here). Credit cards are widely accepted. Central banks ⊕ 09:00–16:30 Mon–Fri. Some branches are open on Sat, but close on Mon; many close 12:00–14:00 for lunch. ATMs are widely available and take most major foreign cards.
American Express: Main Office, ✉ 11 rue Scribe, 9th, ☎ 01 47 77 77 58, **M** Opéra, **RER** Auber, ⊕ 09:00–18:30 Mon–Fri, 09:00–17:30 Sat.
Travelex: ✉ 62 av. des Champs-Elysées, 8th. ☎ 01 42 89 80 32, **M** Etoile.
Also 20 other branches. ⊕ 09:00–21:30 daily.
For lost or stolen credit cards (24 hr):
American Express ☎ 01 47 77 72 00.
Diners Club ☎ 08 10 31 41 59.
Visa/Mastercard ☎ 08 92 70 57 05.

Tipping

Taxi drivers 10 per cent. Restaurant prices include all taxes and service charges, so leave small change only for exceptional service.

Electricity

220V, 2 round pin plugs. Sockets are live, so don't leave things plugged in.

Time

GMT + 1hr in winter; + 2hr in summer.

Toilets

Standards and availability of public toilets have improved greatly in recent years, and most are now squeaky clean. Available in selected metro stations, on the streets in the main tourist areas (often space-capsule style) and in all the cafés and bars, although you need to be quite brave to use these if you haven't bought anything. You may have to walk through the gents to reach the ladies. As ever, life is easier for men; women should keep a stash of coins handy.

Basic Vocabulary

Absolute Basics:

Good morning/afternoon *Bonjour*

Good evening/night *Bon soir/bonne nuit*

Goodbye *Au revoir*

Sir (common usage for all men) *Monsieur*

Madam (common usage for all women) *Madame*

Yes *Oui*

No *Non*

OK *D'accord*

Please *S'il vous plaît*

Thank you (very much) *Merci* (*beaucoup*)

Excuse me/sorry *Pardon*

I don't understand *Je ne comprends pas*

Do you speak English? *Parlez-vous anglais?*

Do you have...? *Avez-vous/Est-ce que vous avez...?*

How much is...? *Combien coûte...?*

When is...? *A quelle heure est...?*

Open *Ouvert*

Closed *Fermé*

Speak more slowly *Parlez plus lentement*

Write it down *Ecrivez-le*

Leave me alone *Laissez-moi tranquille*

Forbidden *Interdit*

Out of service *Hors de service/en panne*

Watch out! *Attention!*

Help! *Au secours/aidez-moi!*

Getting Around:

Where is...? *Où est...?*

Left *Gauche*

Right *Droit*

Straight on *Tout droit*

Railway station *La gare*

Metro station *La station de métro*

Bus stop *L'arrêt du bus*

Platform *Le quai*

Ticket *Le billet*

One-way *Simple*

Return *Aller-retour*

Child's ticket *Un billet d'enfant*

Book of tickets *Un carnet*

Street plan *Un plan*

Map *Une carte*

Calendar:

Monday *Lundi*

Tuesday *Mardi*

Wednesday *Mercredi*

Thursday *Jeudi*

Friday *Vendredi*

Saturday *Samedi*

Sunday *Dimanche*

January *Janvier*

February *Février*

March *Mars*

April *Avril*

May *Mai*

June *Juin*

July *Juillet*

August *Août*

September *Septembre*

October *Octobre*

November *Novembre*

December *Décembre*

Numbers:

Half *Demi/la moitié*

One *Un*

Two *Deux*

Three *Trois*

Four *Quatre*

Five *Cinq*

Six *Six*

Seven *Sept*

Eight *Huit*

Nine *Neuf*

Ten *Dix*

Eleven *Onze*

Twelve *Douze*

Thirteen *Treize*

Fourteen *Quatorze*

Fifteen *Quinze*

Sixteen *Seize*

Seventeen *Dix-sept*

Eighteen *Dix-huit*

Nineteen *Dix-neuf*

Twenty *Vingt*

Thirty *Trente*

Hundred *Cent*

Thousand *Mille*

Travel Tips

In the hotel:

Floor (as in 2nd floor) *L'étage*

Lift (elevator) *L'ascenseur*

Room *La chambre*

Key *La clef/clé*

(Private) bathroom *La salle de bain (privée)*

Bath *Le bain*

Shower *La douche*

Toilet *La toilette; WC*

(Double) bed *Un (grand) lit*

Pillow *L'oreiller*

Air-conditioning *La climatisation*

Heating *Le chauffage*

...does not work ...*ne marche pas.*

Mealtimes:

Breakfast (included) *Le petit déjeuner (compris)*

Lunch *Le déjeuner*

Dinner *Le dîner*

Fixed-price meal *Le menu*

Dish of the day *Le plat du jour*

Starter *Hors d'oeuvres*

Soup *La soupe*

Main course *L'entrée*

Pudding *Le dessert*

Menu *La carte*

Bill *L'addition*

(Fizzy) Water *L'eau (gazeuse)*

Milk *Le lait*

Fruit juice *Le jus de fruit*

Tea *Le thé*

Herbal tea *La tisane*

Hot chocolate *Le chocolat chaud*

Coffee *Le café*

Black *Noir*

With cream *Le café crème*

With milk *Le Café au lait*

Wine *Le vin*

Red/white/rosé *Rouge/blanc/rosé*

Bread *Le pain*

Butter *Le beurre*

Meat *La viande*

Beef *Le boeuf*

Pork *Le porc*

Lamb *L'agneau*

Chicken *Le poulet*

Liver *Le foie*

Kidney *Le rognon*

Sweetbread *Le ris*

Blue (still mooing) *Bleu*

Rare *Saignant*

Medium *A point*

Well-done *Bien cuit*

Fish *Le poisson*

Hake *Le colin*

Trout *La truite*

Prawn *La crevette*

Oyster *La huître*

Snail *L'escargot*

Vegetarian *Végétarien*

Vegetables *Les légumes*

Potato *La pomme de terre*

Chips *Les frites*

Rice *Le riz*

(Green) beans *Les haricots (verts)*

Peas *Les petits pois*

Mixed salad *La salade mixte*

Tomato *La tomate*

Onion *L'oignon*

Lettuce *La laitue*

Cheese *Le fromage*

Ice-cream *La glace*

Apple *La pomme*

Orange *L'orange*

Lemon *Le citron*

Pear *Le poire*

Peach *La pêche*

Apricot *L'abricot*

Strawberry *La fraise*

Raspberry *La framboise*

Etiquette

Life is becoming less formal now, but older people will still wait for permission before using a first name or the familiar 'tu', and invitations into the home only come with a degree of familiarity. Everyone shakes hands on meeting, but the normal greeting among friends is *la bise* – two kisses in central Paris, four in the suburbs and three in many other parts of France.

INDEX OF SIGHTS

GENERAL INDEX

Page numbers given in **bold** type indicate photographs

INDEX OF SIGHTS

INDEX OF SIGHTS